A WEB FOR EVERYONE

DESIGNING ACCESSIBLE USER EXPERIENCES

Sarah Horton and Whitney Quesenbery

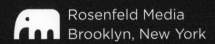

Rosenfeld Media
Brooklyn, New York

A Web for Everyone
Designing Accessible User Experiences
By Sarah Horton and Whitney Quesenbery

Rosenfeld Media, LLC

457 Third Street, #4R

Brooklyn, New York

11215 USA

On the Web: www.rosenfeldmedia.com

Please send errors to: errata@rosenfeldmedia.com

Publisher: Louis Rosenfeld

Managing Editor: Marta Justak

Interior Layout: Danielle Foster

Cover Design: The Heads of State

Cover Illustration: The Heads of State

Artwork for Personas: Tom Biby

Indexer: Sharon Shock

Proofreader: Sue Boshers

ISBN: 1-933820-97-7

ISBN-13: 978-1-933820-97-2

LCCN: 2013944511

Printed and bound in the United States of America

This book is dedicated to the many hardworking and dedicated people for whom a web for everyone is a professional goal, a personal mission, and a daily endeavor.

HOW TO USE THIS BOOK

Who Should Read This Book?

You may be a web or user experience designer, thinking about what makes a product appealing to many people or how to meet the needs of a niche audience. You may be a programmer just handed a list of accessibility coding issues that need repair. You may be a team lead with a mandate from leadership to make accessibility a product differentiator. You might have learned that your organization is under scrutiny from disability rights organizations. You may be an advocate for people with disabilities, looking for ways to make a case for accessibility to a product design team.

No matter your title or skills, you are probably a member of a team that brings together many skills and roles to the task of building products. And you are thinking about accessibility. For accessibility thinking, you need to understand how your work fits with the work of others on your team, and how your decisions and actions affect millions of people around the world who use the web.

This book will help you get started with accessibility or provide a structure for your accessibility thinking. It offers a framework composed of accessible user experience principles and guidelines that will help you create websites and web applications that are accessible for everyone.

What's in This Book?

Chapter 1, "A Web for Everyone," lays out the accessibility equation and a framework of principles and guidelines for an accessible user experience. The framework is formed from three bodies of work: the Web Content Accessibility Guidelines (WCAG 2.0), the Principles of Universal Design, and the concepts behind Design Thinking.

Chapter 2, "People First," introduces a group of personas—realistic but fictional characters that appear throughout the book to show how accessible design can have an impact on people's lives.

Chapters 3–10 cover accessible user experience principles. We start each chapter with an example that demonstrates how the principle is enacted in the "real world" and why it is important for the web. Then we detail how to achieve the principle through supporting guidelines related to strategy, design, content, and coding. We include information about who is responsible and list the relevant WCAG 2.0 principles, guidelines, and success criteria. At the end of each chapter, we profile a leader in the area of accessible design.

The principles are:

- Chapter 3, "Clear Purpose: Well-Defined Goals"
- Chapter 4, "Solid Structure: Built to Standards"
- Chapter 5, "Easy Interaction: Everything Works"
- Chapter 6, "Helpful Wayfinding: Guides Users"
- Chapter 7, "Clean Presentation: Supports Meaning"
- Chapter 8, "Plain Language: Creates a Conversation"
- Chapter 9, "Accessible Media: Supports All Senses"
- Chapter 10, "Universal Usability: Creates Delight"

Chapter 11, "In Practice: An Integrated Process," provides guidance for how to weave accessibility best practices into the fabric of your organization. A web for everyone will become a reality when accessibility is a core value and is considered just part of making things.

Chapter 12, "The Future: Design for All," takes a look at what it might mean to have a web for everyone, before sending you off to your own journey into the future, to play your part.

There are three appendixes. The first is a list of the accessible user experience principles and guidelines in this book, as a handy reference. The second maps the WCAG 2.0 principles, guidelines, and success criteria to the Accessible UX principles and guidelines to help organizations aiming to meet the standard. Finally, there is a comprehensive reading list.

What Comes with This Book?

This book's companion website (rosenfeldmedia.com/books/a-web-for-everyone/) contains some templates, discussion, and additional content. The book's diagrams and other illustrations are available under a Creative Commons license (when possible) for you to download and include in your own presentations. You can find these on Flickr at www.flickr.com/photos/rosenfeldmedia/sets/.

FREQUENTLY ASKED QUESTIONS

I'm not a designer (or I'm not a developer), so why should I read this book?

It's difficult to imagine a context in which one person could take a product, from soup to nuts, and make it accessible. There are so many decisions to be made, and accessibility must be considered at every step along the way. A designer or developer can't make accessibility happen alone.

If the decisions you make as part of your work impact someone's experience of a digital product, you need to know how to make decisions that will not result in accessibility issues.

If you are leading an organization or a team, you may need to shake things up and change how you do business in order to achieve accessibility. You can't just tack it on and hope it sticks. You need everyone to change their processes to make accessibility part of their practice. Chapter 11 looks at putting accessibility into practice.

This isn't part of my job description, so whose job is it?

The simple answer is that we are all responsible for making our part of a project accessible. Rather than try to list all the different roles, titles, and skills, we identify three big groups:

- **Design:** How will we create a great user experience for all?

  Design includes all of the disciplines of UX and web design: information architecture, interaction design, information design, graphic design, and content strategy.

- **Content:** What does the product say, and how does it say it?

  Content includes the ongoing work to plan and produce text, images, audio, video—all the information in the site or app.

- **Development:** How is the product built?

  Development includes programming, coding, scripting, markup, as well as the templates and stylesheets that content authors use.

In Chapters 3 through 10, we identify both who has the primary responsibility for each aspect of accessibility and how all the other roles support it.

How big an issue is accessibility anyway?

The U.S. Census Bureau says that over 47 million Americans have a disability of some kind. The UN and the World Bank say this adds up to 650 million people worldwide. That's around 10% of everyone in the world.

At some point in our lives, disability will affect most of us, no matter who we are, especially as we get older. By the time we retire, over 30% of us will have some disability, even if it is minor.

To put a face on these numbers, we've created a set of personas of web users. They don't represent *everyone*, but they will introduce you to some of the ways people with disabilities use the web. You'll meet them in Chapter 2.

I'm already doing responsive design. Isn't that enough?

Working to standards and responsive design are both important criteria for accessibility. One way to think about accessibility is that assistive technologies, such as screen readers and alternate keyboards, are just another kind of device. When a site is designed to be flexible, it works better on all devices. Chapter 4 covers how to support accessibility with a solid structure.

Accessible UX goes further, to be responsive to differences in people as well as devices. It's about making sure that the ways users interact with your site or application (Chapter 5), navigate (Chapter 6), or read the screen (Chapter 7) allow for user preference.

Is content part of accessibility?

It sure is! There are many reasons why people have trouble reading: cognitive problems like aphasia or dyslexia, physical or vision disabilities, low literacy, or reading in a second language. But even skilled readers can have problems when they are rushed, tired, stressed, or reading on a small screen. Accessible content is written in plain language (Chapter 8) and presented clearly and flexibly (Chapter 7).

Should I follow Section 508 or WCAG?

WCAG 2.0, the Web Content Accessibility Guidelines, is a standard published by the W3C. That means it was created with input from people around the world and reflects the best international consensus. Section 508 is a national regulation in the United States. Other countries and the EU have their own laws and regulations.

If your product is covered by a specific regulation, of course you must meet its requirements. But if you are thinking about accessibility for other reasons, WCAG 2.0 is the place to start. It's a robust standard that is flexible enough to apply in different contexts—websites, desktop apps, mobile apps, even web-enabled teakettles can be measured against the WCAG success criteria.

The good news is that most standards are very similar. The even better news is that the U.S. Access Board (the folks who manage Section 508) has proposed that the next version of Section 508 will use WCAG 2.0 Level AA as its requirements for web content. The EU is also working on new accessibility regulations, and we've been told that they, too, will be based on WCAG 2.0 Level AA. We have our fingers crossed, because in today's global technology world, it would be great to have one standard for web accessibility. You'll find a mapping of the accessible UX principles to WCAG 2.0 in **Appendix B**.

CONTENTS

CHAPTER 6

Helpful Wayfinding: Guides Users   87

CHAPTER 7

Clean Presentation: Supports Meaning   103

CHAPTER 8

Plain Language: Creates a Conversation   125

FOREWORD

 I was an only child, so it shouldn't come as a surprise that I grew up thinking the world revolved around me. In fact, I'll be the first to admit that I was a pretty selfish kid. Well-behaved, certainly, but not terribly concerned with how my actions affected others.

As an only child, the Golden Rule my grandparents insisted was so important—*Do unto others as you would have them do unto you*—didn't really resonate. But I was a kid, what did I know? I was sheltered. I was young. I was the sole beneficiary of my parents' love, time, and money. I had a pretty good life, but I lacked perspective.

I like to think I've grown immensely in the intervening years. Through my work, travel, and moving around a lot, I've experienced dozens of cultures, and I've met hundreds of new people, each with their own life experiences, needs, and desires. Exposure to their unique perspectives has broadened my own and helped me break down the psychological barriers I maintained between me and the "others."

But it wasn't until I started working on the web that I came to a full understanding of the importance of the Golden Rule. Prior to becoming a developer, the ramifications of my decisions were fairly limited. But on the web, every decision I make can have a profound effect on hundreds of thousands (if not millions) of people's lives. I can make checking into a flight a breeze, or I can make it a living hell.

That's a lot of power. And to quote Stan Lee: "With great power comes great responsibility."

My mom always told me that if you choose to do something, you should do it well, so I made it my mission to make the web an easy-to-use, friendly, and accessible place. I chose to make the Golden Rule central to my work.

As schmaltzy and self-aggrandizing as all that may sound, it's also pretty shrewd. The Golden Rule can do wonders for your business. After all, what is good customer service if not treating someone like a human being worthy of your time, consideration, and respect? If we spend every day looking for new ways to make our customers' lives better, we'll create a lasting legacy and build a strong base of customer advocates along the way.

A commitment to universal accessibility is the highest form of customer service. It recognizes that we all have one special need or another at one time or another in our lives, and that fact should not preclude us from experiencing all the web has to offer. It's about providing everyone with equal opportunity to engage with your brand experience, even though they may do so in different ways. It breaks down the barriers between "us" and "them" and recognizes the humanity in our customers.

And it's really not that hard.

In the pages that follow, Whitney and Sarah beautifully lay out the case for accessibility, show you what it looks like, and demonstrate just how simple it is to achieve. They introduce us to a series of personas—Trevor, Emily, Jacob, Lea, Vishnu, Steven, Maria, and Carol—and help us effortlessly slip into each of their shoes, to see the struggles they experience when using the web, and to recognize our own needs and desires in their own.

In a time when many of us are scrambling to keep up with technological advancements and the opportunities they create, this book grounds us in what really matters: people. This book is a roadmap to providing incredible customer service and realizing the Golden Rule in our work and—much like the code we write and experiences we design—the ripple effect it generates is sure to bring about a more equitable web.

Aaron Gustafson
Author, *Adaptive Web Design: Crafting Rich Experiences with Progressive Enhancement*

CHAPTER 1

A Web for Everyone

The web is making the world a smaller and more connected place, but there is still much work to be done to make the web an inclusive place that everyone can use. As web professionals, our decisions define and shape the web landscape. They can create barriers, and they can remove them. Guided by an understanding of people's needs, it's also possible to avoid barriers altogether, right from the start. The approach you take defines whether the web is, indeed, for everyone.

In this book, we will present a design approach that begins and ends with people. We believe that great design starts by thinking about how to make products work for everyone. We will take a broad view, looking beyond the idea of an average user in a typical setting to explore the widest range of user abilities and contexts that we can imagine. Expanding "design thinking" to include all people, we might call it "accessibility thinking," which is using design thinking for accessibility.

Diversity is part of the richness of life. There's even evidence that differences in human brains and how we perceive the world are as essential as biodiversity is to the rich ecosystem of plants and animals.

> Instead of pretending that hidden away in a vault somewhere is a perfectly "normal" brain, to which all other brains must be compared ... we need to admit that there is no standard brain, just as there is no standard flower, or standard cultural or racial group, and that, in fact, diversity among brains is just as wonderfully enriching as biodiversity and the diversity among cultures and races.
>
> Thomas Armstrong, The New Field of Neurodiversity
> **www.alternet.org/story/147107/**

We know that by seeking answers to complex and even singular challenges, we will discover solutions that benefit everyone.

When we have a web for everyone, **people with diverse abilities and contexts can use the web successfully and enjoyably.**

Understanding the Accessibility Equation

Design isn't simply about how something looks. A good design is visually appealing but also meets real needs, has substance and depth, and works well and intuitively.

Designing is an activity. When you make decisions about a product, and your decisions impact the lives of its users, you are *designing*—whether you think of yourself as a *designer* or not. The strategist defines the purpose and goals, the interaction designer focuses on how users will interact with the product, the visual designer creates the look, the content strategist gives the product a voice, and the developer makes everything work. Whatever the title and task, all of these roles are engaged in the activity of design.

When we talk about design, we mean it in this larger sense: the umbrella over all the skills and disciplines that contribute to the user experience.

No matter what your roles or skills are, it's important that you—that all of us—own the term "design" because it comes with incumbent responsibilities, which we need to own as well. Design has the capacity to improve lives. When we wield such a powerful tool, we need to appreciate its power so we are able to use it for good.

Accessibility

Like usability, accessibility is a quality—in this case, it means how easily and effectively a product or service can be accessed and used. Physical and cognitive ability occur along a spectrum. Everyone has a limit as to what they can physically accomplish and intellectually comprehend. Good accessibility is designed for the full range of capabilities, as well as for the context of use or environmental constraints.

As Ben Shneiderman put it in his book, *Leonardo's Laptop*, technology must be designed to include people with "new or old computers, fast or slow network connections, and small or large screens, ... young and old, novice and expert, able and disabled, ... those yearning for literacy, overcoming insecurities, and coping with varied limitations."

When websites and applications are badly designed, they create barriers that exclude people from using the web as it was intended. Poor accessibility creates a disabling environment where the design does not consider the wide variation in human ability and experience. In other words, *disability* is a conflict between someone's *functional* capability and the world we have constructed. In this social view of disability, it is the *product* that creates the barrier, not the *person*, just as design is at fault when a site has poor usability.

We could write this as an equation:

Ability + Barrier = Disability

The question, then, is how to avoid creating barriers and thus maximize the accessibility of a product? The answer: by adopting a practice of accessibility.

When people come first, designers think about real people with real needs. In Chapter 2, "People First," we'll introduce eight mini-portraits of people who use the web and who also happen to have disabilities. Starting with personas like these, you can make sure to design in the necessary features so that everyone has what they need to be successful with your websites and applications.

Think about a building. Public buildings do not generally provide wheelchairs for users with limited mobility. However, they are constructed so that visitors using wheelchairs can get around. Similarly, designers need to anticipate the needs of visitors to their websites and web applications and make sure that the necessary features are available to those who need them.

Inclusive design

Let's go further and think about what it takes to design a great user experience for everyone. We can aim to reverse the equation from one that ends in a barrier to one that includes everyone.

Design + Accessibility = Inclusive Design

A universal web is designed for all, inclusive of geography, language, and culture. It's a place that is available for people of all abilities, aptitudes, and attitudes. In short, design has the power to not only remove barriers but also not to create them in the first place.

The terms *universal design, inclusive design, barrier-free design, human-centered design,* and *design-for-all* are all concepts that strive toward a common goal: to make the user experience the first concern in making design decisions and to expand the description of users to include a wide range of human ability.

Building a Framework for Accessible User Experience

Our goal with this book is an approach that encourages design for everyone, where accessibility is not approached as a last-minute checklist of additions that are piled onto the product, but rather a set of features that are designed in place from the start.

We created a framework, based on established design principles, to identify guidelines and strategies for incorporating accessibility into any website or application throughout the design and development process. The nine principles are:

- **People First: Designing for Differences**

  People are the first consideration, and sites are designed with the needs of everyone in the audience in mind.

- **Clear Purpose: Well-Defined Goals**

  People enjoy products that are designed for the audience and guided by a defined purpose and goals.

- **Solid Structure: Built to Standards**

  People feel confident using the design because it is stable, robust, and secure.

- **Easy Interaction: Everything Works**

  People can use the product across all modes of interaction and operating with a broad range of devices.

- **Helpful Wayfinding: Guides Users**

  People can navigate a site, feature, or page following self-explanatory signposts.

- **Clean Presentation: Supports Meaning**

  People can perceive and understand elements in the design.

- **Plain Language: Creates a Conversation**

  People can read, understand, and use the information.

- **Accessible Media: Supports All Senses**

  People can understand and use information contained in media, such as images, audio, video, animation, and presentations.

- **Universal Usability: Creates Delight**

  People can focus on the experience and their own goals because the product anticipates their needs.

Each principle has a set of guidelines, which we will cover in detail in the following chapters.

To construct this framework, we stand on the shoulders of giants, building on three important bodies of work: the *Web Content Accessibility Guidelines*, the *Principles of Universal Design*, and design thinking.

Web Content Accessibility Guidelines

The Worldwide Web Consortium (W3C) sponsors many efforts in support of accessibility, which is not surprising given the commitment of its founder:

> **The power of the web is in its universality. Access by everyone regardless of disability is an essential aspect.**
>
> **Tim Berners-Lee**
> **W3C Director and inventor of the World Wide Web**

The W3C Web Accessibility Initiative (WAI) develops web accessibility standards and guidelines for web and software developers. The two most important are the Web Content Accessibility Guidelines (WCAG 2.0) and the Accessible Rich Internet Applications (WAI-ARIA) standard. The WAI also provides guidelines for developing web authoring tools (ATAG) and software, like browsers and media players (UAAG).

In addition to standards that are specifically about accessibility, the WAI works with other W3C standards projects, including the HTML5 standard, the next version of the basic language of the web. This standard is critical to making a web for everyone, because there, at the core, is where the basic structures make it easier—or harder—to make a site or application accessible.

The WAI also hosts a great number of educational resources, including the very helpful document, "How People with Disabilities Use the Web" (**www.w3.org/WAI/intro/people-use-web/**).

The Web Content Accessibility Guidelines (WCAG 2.0) are organized under four foundational principles, which conveniently form the acronym POUR:

- **Perceivable:** Information and user interface components must be presented to users in ways they can see or hear.
- **Operable:** User interface components and navigation must be designed so that users can interact with them and they can support assistive technologies such as screen readers.
- **Understandable:** Information and the operation of user interface must communicate clearly and consistently so that the content is readable.
- **Robust:** Content must be written so that it can be interpreted reliably by a wide variety of user agents, including assistive technologies.

Having principles as part of WCAG 2.0 is an important step toward incorporating accessibility into design. Rather than simply following the technical guidelines as a checklist, the principles offer designers an approach to meeting user goals. The principles articulate the "why," and the guidelines articulate the "how" of web accessibility.

We used the POUR principles to think broadly about user needs and WCAG 2.0 to identify the accessible features that must be present in the design. In Appendix B, "WCAG 2.0 Cross-Reference," we map the principles and guidelines to our framework.

Principles of Universal Design

In 1996, a group of designers, architects, and rehabilitation engineers developed a set of principles to support the universal design approach. The approach was based on a philosophy articulated by Ron Mace, an architect, disability rights advocate, and founder of the Center for Universal Design at North Carolina State University.

> **Universal design is the design of products and environments to be usable by all people, to the greatest extent possible, without the need for adaptation or specialized design.**
>
> **Ron Mace**

The Principles of Universal Design start from the premise that there is no typical, average, or normal user. Rather there is a basic understanding that user context will vary widely based on circumstances. With variance as the norm, the principles support a design process that makes sure that any needs arising from differences are met by the design.

- **Equitable Use:** The design does not disadvantage or stigmatize any group of users.
- **Flexibility in Use:** The design accommodates a wide range of individual preferences and abilities.
- **Simple, Intuitive Use:** Use of the design is easy to understand, regardless of the user's experience, knowledge, language skills, or current concentration level.
- **Perceptible Information:** The design communicates necessary information effectively to the user, regardless of ambient conditions or the user's sensory abilities.
- **Tolerance for Error:** The design minimizes hazards and the adverse consequences of accidental or unintended actions.
- **Low Physical Effort:** The design can be used efficiently, comfortably, and with a minimum of fatigue.

- **Size and Space for Approach and Use:** Appropriate size and space is provided for approach, reach, manipulation, and use, regardless of the user's body size, posture, or mobility.

Universal design is appealing because it provides an intentional, designed approach—aesthetic and elegant—while creating products that are often beneficial to everyone. Even though the Principles of Universal Design were written in the early days of the web, the principles and associated guidelines map well to the web environment. As authors, we used these principles to guide our work in the direction of universal access.

You can read the complete universal design principles and supporting guidelines at the Center for Universal Design at **http://tinyurl.com/the-principle-of-universal-des**. You can learn more about universal design in our profile of Valerie Fletcher in Chapter 11, "In Practice."

Design Thinking

Design thinking is an approach to problem solving popularized by Tim Brown from the design firm IDEO. It's based on the idea that the types of thinking and methods behind what we call user experience design benefit all types of decision making processes, and that applying design thinking broadly to challenges and opportunities will produce more successful outcomes.

> **Thinking like a designer can transform the way you develop products, services, processes—and even strategy.**
>
> Tim Brown

The philosophy behind design thinking goes something like this: If you think about technology, you get technological products that don't meet human needs. But if you think more broadly—about the social environment the product will be used in and the people in that setting—you will get products that are truly designed for people.

Several aspects of the design thinking approach are particularly helpful in thinking about designing for accessibility.

- **Integration and iteration:** The full range of design is considered throughout the project, rather than focusing only on the surface layer to make an already conceived product appealing. The entire product is designed by imagining an array of possible approaches; and then, through an iterative process of prototyping and testing, homing in on the best approach based on feedback about the effectiveness of the design.

- **Divergent thinking:** Imagine possibilities without constraints. All too often, accessibility solutions come down to code, without consideration of whether the overall design approach is the right one. Divergent thinking in the early phases of a project, exploring options for accessible designs, yields innovative designs that are also accessible.

- **Convergent thinking:** Choose from all the ideas the ones that are most likely to work, given the environment. This is also important for accessibility: choosing among options the ones that best suit the web environment and meet diverse needs.

- **Human centered:** Design thinking is powered by an understanding of people's wants, needs, and behaviors, which set the direction for a project, as well as feedback from people that helps refine solutions throughout the process.

- **Insight:** To gain human centered insights, you need to understand what works best for people who access and operate the web in different ways. Ideally, this means observing people in their context, watching what they do, and hearing what they say. Stories also generate empathy, which feeds insight. In the next chapter, we'll present personas that we believe will provide the information needed for empathy and insight, and that will inspire creative, divergent thinking about ways to provide accessible solutions.

Using Design Thinking for Accessibility

Design thinking could transform the practice of web accessibility. To date, much of the work on accessibility has focused mainly on modifying code to comply with guidelines and specifications. This approach can only achieve incremental improvements. But applying design thinking to the challenge of accessibility shifts to an innovative approach that could yield substantive new ideas—for example, holistic approaches that incorporate accessibility into design.

In many cases, accessibility is often considered only at the end of the development process, typically during quality assurance or even after launch. Resolving accessibility issues on a finished product often yields unsatisfying solutions, for the designer and the user—the digital equivalent of a wooden ramp stuck on the side of a beautiful building.

A design thinking approach includes accessibility throughout the process. Design thinking also requires going broad and thinking about many different kinds of people in the environment. Instead of designing for a few and then bolting on accommodations for people with disabilities, you can include them in your thinking from the beginning. And with design thinking, you can use your designer's toolkit—exploration, prototyping, and testing—to integrate accessibility into elegant, accessible products.

WCAG + Universal Design + Design Thinking = A Web for Everyone

We'd like to suggest a radical idea: How much more innovative could the web be if everyone used design thinking for accessibility? Instead of limiting creativity, accessibility opens up new avenues for exploration and results in even more awesome products.

Summary

Designing a web for everyone combines good design and usability with accessibility to create inclusive design.

The principles in this book are built on:

- The World Wide Web Consortium's *Web Content Accessibility Guidelines* (WCAG) 2.0, a standard for coding accessible websites. WCAG 2.0 is also the basis for national regulations in the U.S., the U.K., the European Union, and elsewhere. WCAG 2.0's POUR principles provide the foundation for web accessibility guidelines and best practices.

- The *Principles of Universal Design,* seven principles for creating architectural spaces, industrial design, and digital products that work for the widest range of human abilities.

- Design thinking, an approach to solving any kind of design problem that emphasizes grounding the process in understanding the human needs, rather than starting from a technology.

By combining the WCAG guidelines and POUR principles, universal design, and design thinking, and starting from the user experience, you can create websites and web applications that work for everyone—including people with disabilities.

CHAPTER 2

People First: Designing for Differences

It can be hard to think about using the web in ways that are different from your own experience. Your assumptions about use are based on your own experiences with social and work contexts, cultural norms, individual preferences, and your physical abilities. For example, some people can't imagine reading a book without the tactile feel of print; others embrace ebooks both for the new reading experiences they offer and because they fit better into their lives in some way. Similarly, it may be hard to imagine navigating a website without actually seeing where to click.

When designing for differences, **people are the first consideration, and sites are designed with the needs of everyone in the audience in mind.**

Know Your Audience

User experience—including usability and accessibility—starts with users. As Whitney Hess eloquently put it in her blog, *Pleasure and Pain,* "If you design entirely based on intuition without ever gathering intel from a single human being who might at some point in their life come into contact with your business, I'm sorry, but you just aren't a user experience designer."[1]

Those are strong words, but this can't be said strongly enough: You have to know the people you are designing for. And that includes people with disabilities.

It's not as hard as you think. You may find people with a variety of abilities who are already part of your audience.

Be sure to consider the diversity of needs among visitors to your site. In addition to all of the ways the site itself can be formatted for easier access, consider language preferences, literacy or reading habits, and the devices or assistive technology used. Including people with disabilities in user experience design is even easier if you are doing your research or testing online. Most of all, remember that people with disabilities are people first, with habits, context, emotions, and preferences—part of the audience for your work.

User research or usability testing is not just something you do once and check off your list. Keep users in mind throughout the project, using all the UX techniques at your disposal, from early interviews, personas, scenarios, and usability testing.

---

1 http://whitneyhess.com/blog/2011/04/23/youre-not-a-user-experience-designer-if/

One of the best guides to including people with disabilities in user research is Shawn Henry's book *Just Ask: Integrating Accessibility Throughout Design*.

She reminds us to look for users with disabilities who are appropriate for our product:

> *Find people who are fairly experienced using products like yours. If people use assistive technologies with your product, you probably want people who are skilled with their assistive technology. Later in testing, you might want to include some novices, but early on you want people who can teach you well.*

And to consider individual differences, don't just lump all people with disabilities into one user group:

> *People with disabilities are as varied as any users; they come from a variety of backgrounds and have varied interests, likes and dislikes, goals and skills. They have different experiences, different expectations, and different preferences. They use different interaction techniques, different adaptive strategies, and different assistive technology configurations.*

> *Be careful not to assume that feedback from one person with a disability applies to all people with disabilities. A person with a disability doesn't necessarily know how other people with the same disability interact with products, nor know enough about other disabilities to provide valid guidance on other accessibility issues. Just as you would not make design decisions based on feedback from just one user, don't make accessibility decisions based only on the recommendations of one person with a disability. What works for one person might not work for everyone with that disability or for people with other disabilities.*

Just Ask: Integrating Accessibility Throughout Design by Shawn Henry. Available online and in print. **www.uiaccess.com/JustAsk/index.html**

About Personas

To help us think about all the different people who are served by innovative, accessible, universal design, we created eight personas. Personas are a way of combining user research data from many sources into a fictional but realistic character. Personas have names and personal characteristics and abilities, along with aptitudes for using technology, and attitudes about their experiences. They let us look across individuals to see patterns. They are used as stand-ins for all of the real users during the design process so that we remember to put people first, considering how we can make their experience an excellent one.

We'll introduce you to the personas we created for this book. Then throughout the chapters that follow, you will find scenarios and vignettes that illustrate how these personas use the web—and how you can design for them.

To create the personas, we used many public data sources on people with disabilities, from the World Health Organization to the U.S. Census Community Population Survey, to ground the personas in real data.

We have tried to bring some of the statistics and demographic data about people with disabilities to life in the stories of the personas. These stories are based on the many people we have met as colleagues, read about in their blogs, and worked with during user research sessions. And because this is a book about user experience design for the web, we have created personas that are web users. They have the skills, desire, education, and resources to use technology.

No small set of personas can represent the entire world of people with disabilities. It's important to remember that a person with a disability is, first, a person. They like their hometown sports team or love going to the theater. They are funny or quiet, or quick to anger, just like everyone else.

What's in the Personas?

Each persona has a name, a gender, and an age. They all have a personal story about their family, their work, or where they live. These details are not meant to limit the views of the personas, but to anchor them in a realistic setting.

The personas also include information about their abilities, aptitudes, and attitudes, using the model that Ginny Redish and Dana Chisnell developed in their work on how older adults use the web:

- **Ability:** Information about their ability (physical, cognitive, language) and any assistive technology (AT) they use.
- **Aptitude:** Their current knowledge and ability to make inferences.
- **Attitude:** Their motivation, emotion, risk tolerance, and persistence.

Finally, we have identified some of the types of assistive technology they might use and ways in which they might personalize their use of technology.

We hope that these personas will help you connect the technology that accessibility standards support with the people who benefit from its inclusion. Then, for example, when you think about coding for screen readers, you will think of Jacob, or Trevor might give you some insight into cognitive disabilities. Finally, we hope that the goals of the standards will come alive through these characters.

Meet the Personas

In the next pages, we'll introduce you to the personas we created for this book, first in a thumbnail sketch and then in more detail. Throughout the chapters that follow, you will find scenarios and vignettes that illustrate how these personas use the web and mobile devices, giving you some ideas for how to design for them.

Trevor

- High school student with autism
- Likes games and computer worlds
- Poor reading skills and poor social skills; difficulty with visual comprehension

Emily

- Goes to college and works in a community center
- Has cerebral palsy and uses a computer for communication
- Uses a scooter for mobility and has minimal use of her hands

Jacob

- Paralegal with dreams of going to law school
- Proficient with technology; uses computers for "everything"
- Digital native
- Blind since birth

Lea

- Works from home, as an editor and writer for a small magazine
- Uses a split keyboard and dictation software
- Copes with fatigue and weakness from fibromyalgia

Steven

- Graphic artist for a small ad agency
- Uses video chat and texting to connect with anyone else who is deaf or hard of hearing
- Deaf; uses ASL along with interpreters

Vishnu

- Engineer, working on medical technology
- World citizen through technology
- Low vision due to glaucoma
- Uses screen magnifiers and contrast adjustment

Maria

- Community health worker
- Her mobile phone is her first computer
- Uses computer translations
- Needs clearly written information
- Immigrant family is Spanish/English bilingual

Carol

- Grandmother learning to use technology from her grandkids
- Macular degeneration starting to affect her reading ability and slight tremor in her hands
- Has learned to enlarge text in her browser

High school student with autism

I like consistent, familiar places on the web.

Trevor is a bright 18-year-old who plays games and watches music videos on his laptop. He lives at home with his parents and younger sister. He attends a special school where the teachers and staff can help with his social and communication challenges from his Autism Spectrum Disorder, while he works to pass his high school exams.

He has problems with visual information and recognizing things on the page, and his reading skills are not helped by his trouble concentrating on the page or screen long enough to read. His teachers showed him how to make the text bigger on the page, and told him how to use a printable view to hide all the ads with moving images that distract him, because he reads every word on the page very carefully and literally. He can be easily confused by colloquialisms and metaphors. He can also be overwhelmed by sites that offer too many choices.

He likes using the school's forum to talk to his friends. It's easier to just read what they want to say than to listen and try to figure out their facial expressions.

He shares a laptop with the family, but has first dibs on it because his parents want him to get his schoolwork done. He uses it for homework, but he really likes games with repetitive actions. He doesn't like new sites much, in the same way that he doesn't like any changes in his routine: they are tolerated, but not encouraged.

Snapshot of Trevor
- 18 years old
- Lives with family
- Goes to high school
- Computers at school; laptop at home; basic mobile phone with SMS

The A's
- Ability: Autism Spectrum Disorder. Uses larger text and a program that hides everything but the text, so he doesn't get distracted
- Aptitude: Uses the computer well for games, but doesn't learn new sites easily
- Attitude: Prefers familiar sites in an established routine

Assistive Technology
- Text preference settings
- Chat and forums
- Power keyboard user

The Bigger Picture
Source: Autism & Developmental Disability Monitoring Network/CDC

- 1 in 88 children in the U.S. have Autism Spectrum Disorder, ranging from severe to mild social and communications challenges, from classic autism to Asperger's.
- 5 times more boys than girls are diagnosed with ASDs.
- The majority do not have an intellectual disability.

Cerebral palsy, living independently

I want to do everything for myself.

Emily is determined to do things for herself, so she's tried a lot of different keyboards and joysticks over the years, looking for the right kind of interaction. Speech is difficult for her, so she uses a communications program with speech output.

It's slow for her to type with limited use of her fingers. She has stored many phrases and sentences, and can make the program speak for her more easily.

The iPad turned out to be one of the best solutions. Mounted on the scooter, it's always within reach, and touch works better than a keyboard and a joystick. In some situations, it can replace her older communications program.

Instant messaging and social media have also been great. The short formats work well for her, and text can be a more comfortable way to communicate than speech.

Her latest discovery is an app that scans the area to show her what shops and restaurants are in each direction. "I look like a dancing fool spinning my scooter around, but it saves me a lot of time finding someplace new."

Snapshot of Emily
- 24 years old
- Graduated from high school and working on a college degree
- Lives in a small independent living facility
- Works part-time at a local community center

The A's
- Ability: Cerebral palsy, difficult to use hands and has some difficulty speaking clearly; uses a motorized wheel chair
- Aptitude: Uses the computer well, with the right input device; good at finding efficient search terms
- Attitude: Wants to do everything for herself; can be impatient

Assistive Technology
- Augmented & Alternative Communication (AAC) with speech generator
- iPad
- Scooter with joystick control

The Bigger Picture
Source: Harris Interactive/National Association on Disability, "The ADA, 20 Years Later" July 2010, United Cerebral Palsy/National Institute of Neurological Disorders and Stroke

- 800,000 children and adults in the U.S. have one of the forms of cerebral palsy.
- People with disabilities are often unemployed or underemployed. Among all U.S. working age (18–64) people with disabilities, only 21% are employed full- or part-time.

Blind, a bit of a geek

The right technology lets me do anything.

Jacob is a paralegal in a large law firm. He reviews cases and writes summaries, cross-referencing them to the firm's own cases and clients. He's building expertise in his area of law and is hoping to go to law school in a year or so.

As far as Jacob is concerned, it's the technology that's handicapped, not him. When everything is in place, he can work just as fast and just as effectively as anyone in his office.

He's a bit of a gadget geek, always trying out new tools, looking for a little edge and something new. The last few years have been a lot of fun with all the new apps, and VoiceOver on his Mac and phone lets him use most of them pretty well. He likes the challenge of learning new tools.

His other challenge is running. He's training for a 10K run, running with a club in his neighborhood and using an app to plan his routes and track his distance.

He's just started to use The iPhone app, Passbook, and uses it to get train tickets and other travel. The regional rail system has an app, so he can just pull up the barcode and scan it at the ticket office. No fumbling for the right printed card—total independence. Same phone as everyone. Same app as everyone, and it all just works.

Snapshot of Jacob

- 32 years old
- College graduate, legal training courses
- Shares an apartment with a friend
- Paralegal, reviews cases and writes case summaries
- Laptop, braille display, iPhone

The A's

- Ability: Blind since birth with some light perception
- Aptitude: Skilled technology user
- Attitude: Digital native, early adopter, persists until he gets it

Assistive Technology

- Screen reader (JAWS on his laptop, VoiceOver on his phone)
- Audio recorder (to take notes)
- Braille display

The Bigger Picture

Source: World Health Organization, Census

- People with visual disabilities make up about 2.6% of the world's population (about 0.6% are blind).
- In the U.S., about 1.8 million people can't easily see printed words.
- Only about 10% of people who are blind can read and write braille.

Living with fatigue and pain

No one gets that this really is a disability.

Lea was on track to become the editor of the magazine she worked for when she started having numbness in her hands and feeling completely fatigued by the middle of the afternoon. She tried medications and exercise and getting enough sleep, but finally she had to make a change in her life.

She found a job where she could work from home, on her own schedule. When she has good days, it's like nothing is wrong. But on bad days, she measures every action so she can make it through the day. Sometimes that important editorial meeting is all she can manage.

She had to adjust her computer: a new keyboard and trackball make it easier to type, and a good chair helps her avoid tender muscles. The biggest change was learning to write and edit using speech recognition software, Dragon Naturally Speaking.

She's lucky: the company understands that it's a real disability. With an invisible disability like fibromyalgia, some people just don't get it.

Snapshot of Lea
- 35 years old
- Masters degree
- Writes for a trade publication; works from home

The A's
- Ability: Fatigue from fibromyalgia, trackball, and special keyboard
- Aptitude: Average user
- Attitude: Wishes people would understand how hard it can be for her to make it through the day

Assistive Technology
- Split keyboard for less strain on her wrists
- Keyboard controls to minimize arm movement
- Dragon Naturally Speaking

The Bigger Picture
Source: National Institutes of Health http://www.niams.nih.gov/health_info/fibromyalgia/fibromyalgia_ff.asp

- 5 million people in the U.S. have fibromyalgia, 80–90% of them are women.
- People with fibromyalgia and related diseases like lupus, ankylosing spondylitis, and rheumatoid arthritis have increased sensitivity to pain.

Deaf, ASL speaker

My only disability is that everyone doesn't sign.

The nice thing about being a graphic artist is that most of the time his work can speak for itself.

When he first started working, most reviews were done in meetings, but more and more his agency works with clients using online workspaces. He's had some projects recently where all of the communication was through the web. Although he likes seeing live reactions, it's easier for him to participate in the project forum discussions using text rather than audio.

His iPhone has also been important. It was his first phone with a good way to do video chat so he could talk to his friends who sign.

It's annoying when videos on the web aren't captioned. How is he supposed to learn about a new app if the only information is an animated video? Or if he's the only one in the office who doesn't get the joke?

Like many people who learned ASL as their first language, Steven prefers sign, but reads text, since that's most of what the web is. If a site is just a big wall of text, he's likely to leave unless he knows it's got the information he needs.

Snapshot of Steven

- 38 years old
- Art school
- Graphic artist in a small ad agency
- iPad, iPhone, MacBook Pro; good computer at work

The A's

- Ability: Native language is ASL; can speak and read lips; uses SMS/IM, Skype, and video chat
- Aptitude: Good with graphic tools, and prefers visuals to text; poor spelling makes searching more difficult
- Attitude: Can be annoyed about accessibility, like lack of captions

Assistive Technology

- Sign language
- CART—Communication Access Real-Time Transcription—captions for meetings and phone calls
- Captions
- Video chat

The Bigger Picture

Source: Gallaudet University/U.S. Census, audio-accessibility.com

- 10.5 million (3.5%) people in the U.S. are deaf or have a significant hearing loss.
- 500,000 to 2 million people use American Sign Language (ASL).
- Sign is not a universal language. There are national versions around the world, such as Auslan (Australian Sign Language) and three different sign languages in Japan.

Global citizen with low vision

I want to be on the same level as everyone else.

These days, Singapore is a center of the world, and Vishnu is one of its global citizens. After graduating from one of India's technology colleges, he went to a postgraduate program at the National University of Malaysia. His work on visualizing data landed him a job with a multinational medical technology company.

Vishnu was diagnosed with glaucoma and his eyes have been getting steadily worse, despite treatment. He can adjust his monitor and his phone, but many of the technical programs he uses don't have many options, so he has started using a screen magnifier and high-contrast mode.

Like everyone in Singapore, he has several mobile phones. One connects him to his family in India, one is for work, and one is for personal use. He's lucky to have good bandwidth at home and at work. Some of his colleagues from the university live in places with much more erratic connections. Even so, downloading large pages from European or U.S. servers can be slow.

But, if he had one wish, it would be that people would write technical papers and websites more clearly. His English is good, but idiomatic expressions can still be hard.

Snapshot of Vishnu
- 48 years old
- Engineering degree
- Works for a medical software company on projects for international use
- Born in India, finished graduate school in Malaysia, lives in Singapore
- High tech all the way at work; two mobile phones and a laptop for personal use

The A's
- Ability: Speaks three languages: Gujarati, Hindi, English, and a little spoken Mandarin. Uses contrast adjustment to see the screen clearly
- Aptitude: Expert user of technical tools; frustrated searching across languages
- Attitude: Sees himself as a world citizen, and wants to be able to use any site

Assistive Technology
- Contrast adjustments
- Screen magnification software
- Personalized stylesheets for colors that make it easier to read text

The Bigger Picture
Source: The Lighthouse/WHO

- An estimated 135 million people have partial sight.
- Many people in south Asia speak at least three languages: their regional language, Hindi or Mandarin, and English.

Bilingual mobile phone user

I love this. It's all here ... when I can find it.

Maria comes from a traditional Mexican extended family. She grew up helping her parents and older relatives navigate the English-speaking world. Her work as a community health worker is a natural extension. She does outreach and health education in the Spanish-speaking community in LA.

Her husband is good with the computer, and bought one for home, so their kids would be able to use it for their homework. It's become an important way to keep up with their family back home. They post videos of the children and use Skype to keep up with cousins and friends.

Her real lifeline is the smartphone that her family got her last year. Her daughter set up all of her favorite sites in her bookmarks, and she uses the calendar to keep track of her appointments. To tell the truth, she isn't really sure how it all works, but it's wonderful that it does.

She prefers to read in Spanish, especially when she's looking up information that she needs to share with a client in Spanish. Her daughter showed her how to translate a page on the browser. It's not very good, but she can use it to get the general idea of what a page says.

A lot of her professional health education has online videos. Captions help her understand the lectures better, especially for scientific words.

Snapshot of Maria
- 49 years old
- Community college + healthcare certificate
- Married, grown children
- Bilingual (Spanish dominant)
- Community health worker
- Smartphone from her phone service, home computer primarily her husband's, for his business

The A's
- Ability: Prefers Spanish language sites, when she can find them; needs information and instructions written clearly
- Aptitude: Adventurous, but not very proficient; husband and daughter set up bookmarks for her
- Attitude: Thinks it's wonderful to be able to have her favorite websites with her at all times

Assistive Technology
- Skype
- Translation sites

The Bigger Picture
Source: National Center for Health Statistics and U.S. Census, Marketing Charts: http://www.marketingcharts.com/direct/hispanics-more-likely-to-use-new-mobile-devices-17164/

- 17.8 million people in the U.S. speak English "less than well."
- Hispanic U.S. adults are more likely to use mobile devices and mobile search. They are more likely to take mobile pictures and video.

Grandmother with macular degeneration

My grandkids are dragging me into the world of technology.

Carol has always loved reading, so her fading eyesight is a real sorrow to her. She tried recorded books, but she didn't like listening instead of seeing the words in front of her.

As a bookkeeper for 25 years, she made the transition from ledgers to a software program, so she's happy to use the computer. She has an old home computer, which she uses the same way she always did her work—carefully checking everything as she goes. She loves getting emails from her grandkids (and a few friends). She likes reading magazine articles online, especially when they are free. Last year, she discovered that she could get her prescriptions more cheaply online, and now she buys some things from the web.

Her biggest problem is that the text is so small. She's learned how to click on the symbol to make the text bigger, but is frustrated when it doesn't work the same way on every site.

She also finds that her hands aren't as steady as they used to be, and she can't always click on things accurately. She likes her "old fashioned" mobile phone with large buttons that she can feel easily.

As her eyes get worse, she wonders how long she'll be able to keep using the computer. All that light gray text on a white screen. It's just too hard to see. Maybe it's really better for younger people.

Snapshot of Carol

- 74 years old
- Husband passed away a year ago
- Lives in an apartment near one of her daughters, so she can be near some of her six grandkids (ages 6 to 16)
- Graduated from business college
- Retired; worked as a bookkeeper for a construction company for 25 years
- Older computer at home; basic mobile phone

The A's

- Ability: First signs of macular degeneration, mild arthritis; hearing aid; no special AT on computer
- Aptitude: Used computers when she worked as a bookkeeper, but now her grandkids keep her old home computer updated
- Attitude: Willing, but not adventurous

Assistive Technology

- Enlarges text, but little other adjustment

To see what the world looks like with one of nine degenerative eye diseases, download VisionSim from the Braille Institute (for iPhone, iPad, Android) http://brailleinstitute.org/MobileApps/VisionSim.aspx

The Bigger Picture

Sources: CDC, A Nation Online, U.S. Department of Commerce, Braille Institute, Census

- 11 million people in the U.S. have age-related macular degeneration; many more have other forms of degenerative eye diseases.
- After age 65, people have steep increases in disability, with over 59% experiencing a loss of hearing, vision, or dexterity. (U.S. Census says 38% of all adults have disabilities.)

Summary

User experience—including usability and accessibility—starts with users. Personas are a way to combine user research from many sources into realistic characters, to help you remember to put people first during the design process.

This chapter introduces eight personas, differentiated by ability (both physical and cognitive), aptitude (their knowledge and skill with technology), and attitude (their motivation, emotion, risk tolerance, and persistence).

You will hear from these personas in the following chapters, as they help you to understand how different aspects of design affect the success and enjoyment of their experience.

CHAPTER 3

Clear Purpose: Well-Defined Goals

OXO Products

The clarity of the design of the OXO products hides the attention to detail that makes them work so well.

Some of the best examples of purposeful design come from the consumer products company, OXO. Most of their Good Grips line of kitchen tools support a singular task: boil water, peel vegetables, spin-dry lettuce. OXO's products are also designed to be used by people with limited dexterity, such as people with arthritis, and to be comfortable and effective for people who are right- or left-handed.

As an example, consider the travel mug. There are more factors to designing one than you might expect. It helps when you start by thinking about the purpose: to provide a satisfying and safe drinking experience. To design the mug, OXO did research into the "optimal sipping volume" and determined the ideal size and shape to deliver a comfortable amount of hot beverage.

In taking into account the needs of a broad spectrum of users, OXO is able to distill down the critical features of their products to those that are the most necessary and create designs that focus on those features and make their use seem effortless.

It's a happy moment, happening upon a product that has a clear purpose. These products are recognizable by their straightforward effectiveness, dedication to users' goals, a direct path to the task at hand, and freedom from confusing clutter or extraneous elements.

Not many products are able to stick to a singularity of purpose—it takes restraint on the part of the designer and the consumer. It's easy to fall into the trap of creating multi-featured tools, like the Veg-O-Matic: "It slices, it dices! But wait, there's more!"

A clear purpose helps to create designs that avoid unnecessary complexity. Guided by the goal to deliver content and functionality to the broadest possible audience, teams have the means to stay true to the product purpose and make design decisions that favor the most universally usable approach.

How Clear Purpose Supports Accessibility

A clear purpose is a key to good user experience *and* accessibility. Sprawling, cluttered websites and complex, multi-layered web applications are harder for everyone to use. By maintaining focus on essential features and functionality and favoring simple solutions, designs are better for everyone.

With a clear purpose, **people enjoy products that are designed for the audience and guided by a defined purpose and goals.**

- **Sites can be less complex and confusing.** Pages with many different "calls to action" and competing content can be especially difficult for people who have difficulty focusing or an attention deficit disorder.

- **Page layouts are clear.** If the purpose is not clear, it's hard to have a clean hierarchy of information in either the visual design or underlying structures. Clean layouts work better for people who use screen magnification software and can only see a portion of the screen at a time. Simpler pages are also easier for people who don't read well or are reading the language of the page as a second (or third) language.

- **Forms and other sequential interactions make sense.** Many types of assistive technology present web pages in a linear sequence. Layered interactions that are not coded clearly can be difficult for people who are not frequent web users (and may be less comfortable exploring) and can be impossible for people using assistive technology to navigate.

- **Accessibility can be built in.** Fixing problems in a design never works as well as avoiding them to begin with. And fixes made late in a process often require changes that compromise the design. When the purpose is clear, design, code, usability, and accessibility can work together from the beginning.

Maria

When a site is confusing, I just leave.

My clients, most don't speak English well, so I need sites that have health information in Spanish, too. I can read it with them and make sure that they understand it, and that they know the words to tell their doctor.

To tell you the truth, on my own, I don't stay on a site long if it's confusing. On many sites, there is so much crammed in that I can't find anything at all. It just makes my head hurt to even try. I like the sites that are simple and don't have so many decisions I have to make. When I find a site that works for me, I stick to it. I have a nice health site that I use most of the time. For anything else, I just search.

How to Design for a Clear Purpose

Design for universal usability is an excellent way to arrive at a clear purpose. You can focus on necessary features, avoiding elements that are not essential to the product purpose. With accessible design as a starting point, you end up with a better product—one that has a clear purpose and is easier for everyone to use.

Start with purpose and goals

All too often, teams dive into a project without a clear idea of its purpose and goals. They start knowing the site will have a shopping cart, video, or social media, and then dive into designing the site without first knowing its core mission.

When considering the purpose and goals, focus on audience goals rather than business goals. In most cases, using a product isn't a goal in itself, so dig deeper and see what needs it will meet. For example, "use social media," is not a user goal, but rather "connect with my friends," or "let the world know what I'm doing," or even "tell my family that I'm on my way home."

The design team should be able to answer the questions, "Why does this website exist?" and "What value does this site provide for the people who use it?" It's easy to get excited about technology ideas or get bogged down in lists of features. But teams that work from a shared understanding of the clear purpose for a product make better decisions about features and functionality.

Design for clarity and simplicity

The digital environment is incredibly flexible—seemingly without boundaries. However, each new feature adds complexity and can adversely impact usability. And bad general usability can mean *no* usability for people with disabilities.

Try focusing design and developmental efforts on critical aspects of the product—the content and functionality required for the product to achieve its purpose. Even when working on a complex product, look for ways to make it *appear* simple. When you can explain the purpose of the site or app clearly, it's easier to choose among design options.

Four Strategies for Simplicity

In his book *Simple and Usable*, Giles Colborne identifies four strategies for simplicity:

- **Remove:** Get rid of unnecessary elements until the product has only the essentials.
- **Organize:** Arrange the elements on the screen so that they make sense.
- **Hide:** Move any elements not essential for mainstream use so that they do not clutter the screen.
- **Displace:** Consider whether any elements or features can be handled off-screen, either in a different part of the site, on a different device, or by users themselves.

www.simpleandusable.com

Think "accessibility first"

The best time to consider accessibility is at the start of a project when defining the product purpose. When accessibility is part of the purpose and built in from the beginning, the product works better for everyone.

This way of thinking may seem backward. Why start with the exceptions? Historically, websites and web apps have been designed for early adopters, then adapted for a more general audience, and only then made accessible, usually imperfectly.

When good designers shift this around, thinking about accessibility first, they end up with a product that is stronger and more usable for everyone. Considering a diverse audience is just the same as working in many languages or across many devices and platforms. When you include accessibility in your thinking from the beginning, it is just one more aspect of the flexibility needed for today's products.

Emily

Simpler screens are easier screens.

I love having a tablet computer. It's small enough to go everywhere with me. However, being small can also mean that the whole page gets small and crowded, and that makes it harder for me to use the site. I can't tell you how often I've gone zooming off to the wrong link or couldn't hit the right button. The ones I like seem to have everything in the right place. It's like they read my mind and put the things I need on the screen when I need them.

Designing for Mobile Helps Focus on What Matters

As the web moved to smaller mobile devices, designers like Luke Wroblewski saw an opportunity to shift the paradigm and make a move toward simplicity. Websites can be flexible. You can add menus, link in new pages, and add more widgets pretty easily, especially compared to older software engineering. As screens got bigger and the Internet got faster, optimizing a site was not as big a problem. That led to feature creep. Instead of being even more rigorous about what is important enough to get space at the top of the page, pages got bigger and the text got smaller, to cram more onto the screen. Something had to give.

Luke suggested that design start with "mobile first." Instead of trying to cut down a large website, you can use the constraints of a small screen to make the hard decisions about how to use the precious real estate on a mobile screen. The discipline required to build a good mobile experience also forces you into a simpler approach overall, without unnecessary complexity and with important information first.

You can see a video of Luke's talk about his approach from the LinkedIn Tech Talk series at **www.lukew.com/ff/entry.asp?1137** or read his book, *Mobile First*.

Make templates accessible, too

Templates, widgets, and toolkits are the building blocks for many websites. Even experienced developers usually start from a template or sample code. The effort to make templates accessible pays off every time they are used, and sites built from accessible templates work better for everyone.

For example, WordPress is one of the largest content management systems out there. According to wordpress.org, it's built by a community of volunteers, and is used by over 25 million people to build a site or a blog. The default WordPress 3.0 theme was called Twenty Ten, and it looks like the screen in Figure 3.1.

Like all of the WordPress themes, it's a fully designed site that's ready for an author to customize with different headers, menus, and widgets.

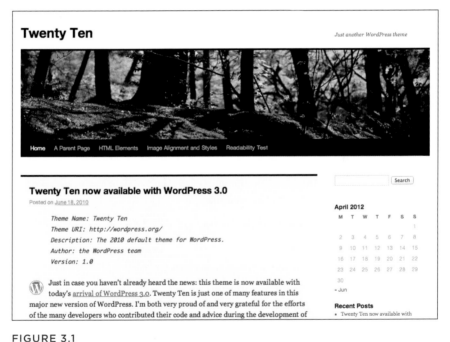

FIGURE 3.1

WordPress Twenty Ten theme: http://2010dev.wordpress.com/

Now, let's take a look at an accessible version of Twenty Ten in Figure 3.2.

FIGURE 3.2
Accessible WordPress modified Twenty Ten theme: http://accessible.
sprungmarker.de/2011/01/accessible-1-0/

For this variation (or child theme), the designer, Sylvia Egger, added a few features to make the site accessible:

- Accessible color contrast meeting WCAG AAA
- Better keyboard handling with visible focus
- Link hover and active states so it's easier to see
- Skip to content links at the top
- Headings for sidebars to help identify the content

That's it. And you can barely tell the difference in the overall look of the design.

Even better, volunteers are working to include features that support accessibility in the standard WordPress themes. With thousands of people using a theme, a few extra steps will make all the sites created with it work better for everyone. Because whether they need large text and high contrast to read easily, use a keyboard to jump from link to link, or control their computer with voice input, everyone comes to those sites with the same goals: to read, explore, learn, or shop.

Choose an accessibility strategy

Accessibility is not black and white, on and off. You should aim for full accessibility, but when you hit roadblocks, it's helpful to think about a range of approaches, listed here from most to least desirable.

- **Universal (or inclusive) design—one site.** Everyone has the same means of use, with elements that work for everyone, no matter what interaction mode is chosen. The goal of this book is to help you create universal or inclusive websites and apps, so no one is left out of the experience. For example, a video with captions and video description and an accessible video player lets everyone watch the same video.
- **Equivalent use—includes alternatives.** Products contain similar ways to meet the same goals but present them in different ways. For example, a transcript for an audio file has the same information, but someone reading the information has a different experience than someone listening to the audio.
- **Accommodation—a separate "accessible" version.** Accommodation is disability-speak for working around a barrier without removing it—"separate but not equal." Accommodations like a "text only" version are not acceptable. It's not okay to create a separate design—one that delivers a separate and degraded experience—for people with disabilities.

Who Is Responsible for Clear Purpose?

A clearly defined purpose forms the basis for projects and serves as a touchstone throughout the project. Every member of the project team needs to be on board with that purpose and remain loyal to it. Design for clear purpose is a guiding principle through all phases of the design process.

In his book, *Brunelleschi's Dome*, Ross King describes how the Florence Cathedral got the largest masonry dome ever built. For 50 years, master builders were required to swear an oath that they would follow the model as they built the church, even though no one at the time had the slightest idea how to build a roof that large. Each master builder took up the challenge, solving one problem after another, until they were able to complete the project. That's faith in a project vision.

Equivalent or Accommodation: Easy Chirp and Twitter

As wonderful as Twitter is, it is clear that it was not built with universal design in mind. Compare the Twitter client (Figure 3.3) with an accessible version (Figure 3.4).

The Twitter website was designed for use on a large display. It puts a lot of functionality in a small space. But it's not designed or built for accessibility. Although the Twitter site has been redesigned several times, it's still hard for some people to use.

Easy Chirp takes advantage of the Twitter application programming interface (API) to create an accessible site. It's not pretty, but Dennis Lembrée designed it for access by anyone, regardless of ability and using any web interface. It has all of the functionality of the Twitter website, coded so that it works with screen readers.

The difference between these two ways of using Twitter is immediately clear. There are two ways to look at this from a universal design perspective.

FIGURE 3.3
Twitter website:
www.twitter.com.

First, you might ask why Twitter didn't think that it was important to work for screen readers. Twitter made sure that it was globalized, working in dozens of languages. Why not make sure that it worked for screen readers?

But you can also look at the fact that there is a robust API. There are many programs that help people work with Twitter in their own way. In this view, Easy Chirp is just another variation for people with particular needs.

The danger of taking advantage of this "equivalent use" approach and relying on other programs for accessibility is that they all have to be kept up-to-date as features and the API change. Over time, the accessible versions can fall behind or even stop working entirely. This happened to Easy Chirp when Twitter changed its API in early 2013. As this book went to press, Dennis Lembrée announced the launch of Easy Chirp 2 with help from Kickstarter funders.

What do you think?

FIGURE 3.4
Easy Chirp website
in early 2013:
www.easychirp.com.

Summary

A clear purpose is the starting point for any successful design. Like any user experience design, a clear purpose starts with understanding the audience, including people with disabilities.

Thinking about accessibility from the beginning—"Accessibility First"—is similar to the approach of thinking "Mobile First" to ensure that the design works as well in a screen reader as it does on a small screen.

There are three approaches to accessibility:

- Universal design aims for a website or app in which the same design and content elements work for everyone, no matter how they interact with the web.

- Equivalent use focuses on ensuring that each mode of interaction—visual or auditory, tactile or keyboard, for example—has an equally good experience.

- Accommodation is the least desirable, because it creates a separate—and usually unequal—experience.

Giles Colborne is co-founder of cxpartners, a design consultancy specializing in strategy- and research-driven approaches for designing websites and web applications. With a rigorous practice of user research and usability testing, cxpartners creates simple, easy-to-use designs, paying particular attention to global accessibility.

In his book Simple and Usable: Web, Mobile, and Interaction Design, *Giles teaches the art and science of achieving simplicity in interface design. We wanted to learn from Giles how accessibility can impact a simple, purposeful design approach, and vice versa.*

Simplicity is good science and good interface design.

Giles comes to interface design from science. As a physics student, simplicity was impressed on him as the mark of good science. "The whole purpose of the scientific endeavor is to pack reality back down into a handful of equations." He credits his background for his enthusiasm for approaching a seemingly complex interface challenge and seeking the path to the simplest solution. "It doesn't strike me as paradoxical, it strikes me as rather beautiful."

In practice, most interfaces we encounter don't reflect Giles' enthusiasm for simplicity. "People make software very difficult to use by loading on features." The result is software that requires practice to become proficient.

Simple designs put complexity in its place.

In one project, Giles worked on improving the interface for a travel planner. The software tapped into a vast store of data, of places to see and things to do, with supporting details about location, time to get there, time needed to visit, and hours of operation. "When we put the interface together, it totally bombed. The app was constantly saying, 'You can't do this, you can't do that, you haven't done enough of this.' It was so hard to use, and so unforgiving."

Giles went back to the drawing board. Rather than have the software identify possible options, he had users create lists of locations and places that were of interest to them. The computer didn't try to work out whether or not the itinerary was practical—it gave people enough data to figure it out themselves.

> *People are good at imagining the future. Computers are good at remembering stuff. By handing off the task of imagining to the user and the task of remembering to the computer, it all worked out. The process taught me a powerful lesson about where complexity belongs, who should own it.*

profile continues on next page

Observe real people to learn what's needed.

Giles' practice is informed by user research. "You can't make safe predictions about how things are going to work until you engage with the audience." And that means engaging with real people, not through imagined personas or user stories.

People fall in love with pen portraits of their users. Not their real users—the users they'd like to have: young, attractive, happy, active, outdoorsy, not distracted, completely able-bodied. When you bring real users to the testing and design process, the reality is that there's much more variability.

Giles finds that some of the greatest insights come from studying how people work in extreme circumstances. For one project, Giles researched how people with ADHD manage their condition as a way of understanding more broadly how to design for distracted users.

Everyone operates under some kind of duress that degrades their performance, and yet we design stuff in nice quiet offices and reflect on the design and interface and take a long time discussing something that a user needs to do in a fraction of a second.

Giles does international testing, which also yields insights that resonate with accessibility. A design that can adapt from English to Chinese must handle enlarged text, so small details in the characters are legible. "That flexibility in presentation is at the core of what you're thinking about when you're thinking about designing for accessibility."

Designing for multiple devices supports accessibility.

Giles has seen significant change in how design is done, due to the diversity of devices. Instead of detailed wireframes and mock-ups, now he starts with information hierarchies. Instead of creating Photoshop mock-ups, prototypes are done in code, with designs and layouts that respond to different viewports. This change in practice may move us closer to designs that are simple and usable, for everyone.

As soon as you start to think about how navigation appears on a small screen, you start to focus on information hierarchies that also work well for accessibility. On a small screen, you don't want navigation, and then you scroll down and there's content. You want content, and then scroll down and there's navigation. And, of course, that's what you want for a screen reader as well. This discipline of designing for multiple platforms and environments makes you start to think in useful ways about accessibility.

CHAPTER 4

Solid Structure: Built to Standards

Solid Ramps and Infuriating Ramps

Two wheelchair ramps show the value of good structure and building to standards.

Personal experience provides cues as to whether a physical structure is built well or looks unsafe because of obvious construction details, such as where the structure is placed or how it feels under our feet.

Wheelchair ramps provide a lot of examples of both obvious structural integrity and ramps that make you wonder what their designers were thinking. You can see the difference between the two in the illustration on this page: the one on the right suggests a solid structure, while the one on the left looks ramshackle, difficult, and dangerous.

The digital environment does not currently have an equivalent to the rigorous building codes and legal requirements of civil engineering and architecture. As we all come to appreciate the impact of digital products on health, safety, and general welfare, we are likely to see more interest in standards and certification in this area.

When navigating the physical environment—public spaces in particular—we take structural integrity for granted. As a rule, we don't usually have to think about whether the entry ramp at a building will collapse. In fact, we assume that it was designed and built to specifications, and that the people responsible for safety have set requirements that will make the ramp safe, sound, and accessible. However, when we see cues that this is not the case, we worry.

For websites and applications, "structural integrity" means software that does not break or have system failures. It also means a site that does not break in all its different contexts of use, including all the ways that users can customize their own experiences. For universal design, a site with a solid structure is one that does not create barriers in how it is constructed, but can be used by everyone.

Master builders know that crafting each element with care—even things that are never seen or directly experienced—is important. Quality and stability depend on care and precision at all levels. Taking this same approach with the code beneath the surface of a website or web application makes for a more stable design. It also has an impact on accessibility, because the way that code is written can dictate the quality of the user experience.

How Solid Structure Supports Accessibility

Although websites are created for people, every web page requires code. Tim Berners-Lee conceived the Internet as "a web of data that can be processed directly or indirectly by machines."[1] Machine-readable data is what makes the web so powerful.

Programming instructions and markup add a layer of information by describing the content of the site and providing instructions for interaction. For example, HTML heading tags instruct software that the text element is a heading that describes the subsequent section.

Machine-readable data with instructions for its use paves the way for assistive technology—software and hardware that transform and adapt websites and web applications for different modes of use.

With a solid structure, **people feel confident using the design because it is stable, robust, and secure.**

---

1 Berners-Lee, T. *Weaving the Web*. HarperCollins, New York, NY, 1999.

- **Sites work across devices and technologies.** To work correctly, assistive technology has to be able to accurately read the underlying code to identify and communicate all of the features of a website or web application to the user. Standards-based code that adheres to accessibility guidelines improves accuracy.

  People routinely use websites on different devices—from large screens to tiny ones, and on different operating systems—from Windows to iOS. Assistive technology is just another device. People also interact with sites in different ways. Touch, keyboard, audio, and speech are all useful at different times. A strong structure allows consistency and flexibility across devices and interaction modes so that everyone has an equitable experience.

- **Sites are more trustworthy.** Even though the underlying structures are not always immediately visible, like good bone structure, they show up in the "skin" of the user experience. People with disabilities encounter so many broken experiences that they may be hesitant to even try a site that doesn't have clear signs that it is structured to support assistive technology.

- **User needs and preferences are met.** No matter how well you do your design research, you cannot design for every person in every situation. When the product is designed to be flexible, it allows users to customize the display and interaction without breaking the design.

Jacob

This makes it possible to do my job.

They say that on the Internet, no one knows who you are. That's really true for me. I think there are people in my company who don't know I'm blind—they only see me through email or the case summaries I write. When a site works with my screen reader, I have control over my own experience. I can preview the content on the page by listening to all the headings on the page. I'm confident I know I'm putting the right information in the right field on a form. Best of all, I'm no different from anyone else—and I'm faster than some of my co-workers, if you want to know the truth.

When a website is not accessible, or I run into broken links or forms, it's really frustrating. Sometimes I miss important information because it's hidden from my screen reader. Or I have to spend a lot of time figuring out what's going on. I just want to be able to do things for myself, and when sites are broken, I can't.

How to Create a Solid Structure

The web can be very forgiving, allowing sites with sloppy code to function ... sort of. But those sites aren't very robust and may only work with specific browsers. Paying attention to the underlying code so that it works well for both people and other technology is the key to strong sites.

Code content to be machine-readable

Web accessibility relies on the software's ability to read and understand the content and instructions contained in web pages. When the code includes all the markup and tags to communicate meaning accurately, the information on the page is *programmatically determinable*, and a browser or other device can read and act on it.

Elements in a web experience that the software cannot read produce barriers, which are indecipherable and therefore inaccessible. The more "meta" information you can provide, the better the user experience will be, since software can do more with information it can parse and act on (see Figure 4.1).

```
<h1>Solid Structure: Built to Standards</h1>

<h2>How to create solid structure</h2>

<h3>Code content to be machine-readable</h3>
```

FIGURE 4.1
Heading tags (<h1...6>) communicate the information structure described by the tags to browsers and assistive technology software.

Code to standards

Coding standards are the building codes of the digital environment. They provide the tested and approved specifications that allow websites to work across different versions of browsers and different devices. Without standards, we would have the chaos of the early years of the web, in which every browser worked differently, so websites were full of "hacks" to make them work. The result was inconsistency and instability—websites that looked fine in one browser and a mess in another.

The choice for the developer is either to code browser- and platform-specific versions or exclude visitors who arrive using a non-preferred system. ("This site is best viewed using Internet Explorer for Windows.")

This chaos is not good for websites in general, but it's really bad for accessibility.

You may be already coding to standards. If so, you are well on the way to creating accessible sites and applications. If you aren't, or if your development tools don't help you produce compliant code, now would be a good time to start. Table 4.1 shows the most relevant coding standards and guidelines for accessible web sites.

TABLE 4.1 STANDARDS FOR THE WEB

HTML (Hypertext Markup Language)	Language for describing the structure of a page, including semantic information, for including interactive links and forms, and for embedding media elements such as images and video. **www.w3.org/html/**
CSS (Cascading Style Sheets)	Language for describing the presentation aspects of a page, including color, type, and layout. **www.w3.org/css/**
JavaScript (officially known as, ECMAScript)	Scripting language for providing interaction and dynamic content. **www.ecma-international.org/**
WCAG 2.0 (Web Content Accessibility Guidelines)	Guidelines and techniques for making websites and web applications accessible to people with disabilities. **www.w3.org/WAI/**
WAI-ARIA (Accessible Rich Internet Applications Suite)	Framework for adding attributes to web documents in order to make actionable elements accessible to people using assistive technology. **www.w3.org/WAI/intro/aria**

Coding to standards means writing accurate code that passes validation for the appropriate technology standards, including HTML and CSS. An automated accessibility validation check against web accessibility guidelines can help identify coding issues that affect accessibility. However, accessibility has many subjective aspects that cannot be fully tested by software. You can use accessibility checkers as a tool, but you should not rely on the results to ensure accessibility. (See the list of validation tools in Appendix C, "More Reading," and in *Provide tools and assistive technology for ongoing evaluation* in Chapter 11, "In Practice.")

There are two organizations that provide important support and guidelines and best practices to help ensure that sites have a solid structure.

Web Accessibility Initiative (WAI): A project of the Worldwide Web Consortium (W3C). WAI produces guidelines for accessible websites and web applications, notably:

- Web Content Accessibility Guidelines (WCAG)
- WAI-ARIA, the Accessible Rich Internet Applications Suite

WAI also produces guidelines for software that accesses websites and web applications, and for software used to build sites and apps:

- User Agent Accessibility Guidelines (UAAG) for web browsers and media players
- Authoring Tool Accessibility Guidelines (ATAG) for software that creates websites
- A new WAI project, IndieUI (Independent User Interface), is working to create a device-independent way to communicate user actions, such as scrolling, to a web application.

Using W3C and WAI guidelines and techniques is a roadmap for building accessible websites and web applications (**www.w3.org/wai**).

The Web Standards Project (WaSP): An advocacy group of leading designers and developers "fighting for standards that ensure simple, affordable access to web technologies for all." For its 15 years, WaSP had a significant impact in getting browser software to do away with custom code and instead support standard technologies, which in turn has allowed developers to code to standards. This project shut down in March 2013, saying that its work was done, and it was time for everyone to ensure that the web remains free, open, and interoperable (**www.webstandards.org**).

Use standard web technologies

In addition to coding to standards, it's important that you select the right technologies to use. A sure sign of structural integrity is the ability to function in different contexts and on different devices. If you use technologies that aren't widely supported, your product won't work in many situations, causing problems for all users. For example, if your product is coded in Flash, people using an iPad or iPhone will only see a box indicating content that is not supported in Apple iOS.

Look for technologies that are widely supported by browsers and assistive technologies, without the need for plug-ins. If you find yourself planning to use a technology that requires a plug-in, such as Flash, Flex, Silverlight, or QuickTime, you might be able to implement the functionality more simply using standard web technologies. (See "Guidelines for Rich Internet Applications in Flex, Flash, and Silverlight" in Chapter 5, "Easy Interaction.")

Organize code for clarity and flow

In visual design, pay attention to where elements appear, featuring important information prominently, near the top, and putting more incidental information at the bottom of a design. Location matters in visual communications, along with other factors such as size, color, and alignment.

In source code, order, or the sequence of elements in the code, influences how software reads a page and, in turn, how well software conveys information to the user. Web browsers generally—and screen readers, in particular—start reading at the top of a page and read through the code sequentially. The order of the source code makes a difference to search engines, too. They treat headings and information at the top of the page as more relevant. If it's more important, of course, it's at the beginning of the page!

Coding is as much a craft as any other kind of writing. To craft readable code, you can organize the code in an inverted pyramid so that the most important content and functionality is at the beginning of the file, near the top of the page code. Content that appears "above the fold" in code will be what gets read first by the software (see Figure 4.2).

You should also make sure that the sequence of related elements is not broken by unrelated elements. Consider how elements that are closely related are sequenced. For example, a label for a text input field should appear in the code before its input element (as well as being connected to it by using the label tag), and an image caption should appear in the code after its image.

Provide accessible instructions and feedback in Chapter 5 covers sequencing and how it affects interaction. For solid structure, you should code important information first and follow a logical, unbroken flow.

FIGURE 4.2

Wikipedia puts the page content in the code before the top and side navigation, where assistive technology can read it first. http://en.wikipedia.org/wiki/Jelly_bean

Sectioning markup is a way of associating a group of elements programmatically and then giving them a label. When the purpose and function of elements is encoded into a page, software can use that information to, for example, move focus between different sections, or jump directly to one section, such as navigation or search. HTML, HTML5, and WAI-ARIA provide markup that allows you to draw a virtual bounding box around a group of elements and label their relatedness in the code. For example, the HTML <fieldset> tag allows you to identify and label a group of form elements as "Contact Information."

You can use sectioning markup for main sections of the page, such as the HTML5 <nav> tag or the ARIA attribute role="navigation" to mark site navigation. Be sure to use sectioning markup wherever possible to improve the readability and navigability of your code. (Table 4.2 and *Provide clear landmarks within the page* in Chapter 6, "Helpful Wayfinding," have more details on using sectioning markup.)

TABLE 4.2 SECTIONING MARKUP TO GROUP AND LABEL

HTML	body, fieldset, form, table (thead, tbody, tfoot), lists (dl, ol, ul), div
HTML5	article, aside, footer, header, main, nav, section
WAI-ARIA	application, banner, complementary, contentinfo, form, main, navigation, search

Use stylesheets to separate content and presentation

The architecture of a web page has two layers: content—the text, images, tables, lists, and so on—and presentation, which includes the color, font, layout, and so on. The content layer is typically contained in the HTML code.

The correct standards way of specifying the presentation layer is with Cascading Style Sheets (CSS). Using CSS, all of the information about how to present the page is stored in a separate file, which can be used by many web pages. There are two advantages to using stylesheets:

- The separation of content and presentation generally simplifies coding. The HTML can be clean, without being cluttered, with display instructions. Changes to the presentation can be implemented across multiple pages by changing the central CSS document.

- The site can adjust to different displays or screen sizes, either with alternative presentations in the stylesheet, or by substituting one that is more appropriate for the display. Print stylesheets, for example, can set up a page for printing. Using a stylesheet also makes it possible to customize the presentation without breaking the site. Users can set their own colors, font size, or layout to match their own preferences or visual needs.

The customization enabled by using CSS can be as simple as making the text larger, or as extreme as a whole new look. Figure 4.3 shows how one site can have very different looks. We'll look at the presentation layer in detail in Chapter 7, "Clean Presentation."

Use semantic markup for content

Semantic markup makes information meaningful to software. And when software can read and make sense of information, wonderful things happen for those of us who use the software. Take search, for example.

Search engine software reads and catalogs a document based on determinations about subject and focus. It reads the title as a strong indication of the topic of the page, and it gives text tagged as headings more weight than other text. The inclusion of these semantic tags, `<title>` and `<h1...6>`, improves the software's accuracy in cataloging, which, in turn, improves your ability to find what you are looking for when using search.

FIGURE 4.3

CSS Zen Garden is David Shea's demonstration of what can be accomplished visually through a CSS-based design. These three pages all use the same HTML file. Designers from around the world have created their own stylesheets to display the page in their own way. (www.csszengarden.com/)

FIGURE 4.4

List of headings from the JAWS screen reader. en.wikipedia.org/wiki/Jelly_bean

Headings are particularly important, because most screen readers provide a helpful list of headings on a page so that users can use them to navigate the hierarchy of information. In the 2012 WebAIM survey of people who used screen readers (**webaim.org/projects/ screenreadersurvey4/**), 61% reported that the first thing they did on a page was to scan the headings using the navigation tools in their assistive technology.

Figure 4.4 shows an example of the list of headings for a Wikipedia page in the JAWS screen reader. Notice in this example that many headings begin with "[edit]." This is because Wikipedia has coded the section edit link within the heading tag, with the unfortunate result that the headings are difficult to scan. Chapter 7 has more about writing good, scannable links and headings.

Semantic markup describes the purpose of individual elements in the information (a paragraph, a heading, a citation, a quote) or group-related elements (a set of form fields, a table of data). By reflecting organization and meaning in the code structure, semantic tags make content stronger and easier for browsers and assistive technology to read.

For example, marking text with the emphasis tag (<em>) communicates the importance of the words, just as changes in the visual presentation do.

Semantic markup communicates meaning, but does not specify the presentation.

```
<em>Never</em> put your hands in the blender <em>while it is
    turned on</em>.
```

The same markup can have different visual presentations, based on styles that interpret the markup.

Never put your hands in the blender **while it is turned on.**

Never put your hands in the blender **while it is turned on.**

Never put your hands in the blender **while it is turned on.**

We'll look at writing content for accessibility in more depth in Chapter 8, "Plain Language."

Who Is Responsible for a Solid Structure?

Structural integrity is primarily the responsibility of the people who write the code that produces the website or web application. Although this layer is invisible to most users, the underlying code has a profound impact on accessibility.

But the entire team plays a part, right from the beginning, by thinking about how each decision affects the ability to code to standards. As the design begins to take shape in the form of sketches, models, and wireframes, take the time to consider whether the emerging user experience concepts lend themselves to coding to standards, and thus to good accessibility for your users.

Taking the time at the beginning to consider the impact of technical decisions will result in fewer problems later in the project when structural flaws are more difficult and costly to repair.

WCAG 2.0 and Solid Structure

The guidelines for Solid Structure relate to the following WCAG 2.0 requirements.

Solid structure makes the site **Robust**, coded so that it can be read by a variety of browsers and other technologies for accessing the web, including assistive technologies. It is also **Perceivable** because content structure and relationships can be read by technology. (Robust and Perceivable are two of the four foundational POUR principles for the Web Content Accessibility Guidelines, described in Chapter 1.)

A site with solid structure meets **Guideline 4.1: Maximize compatibility with current and future user agents, including assistive technologies.**

The requirements for solid structure are:

- **1.3.1 Info and Relationships:** Information, structure, and relationships conveyed through presentation are also either explained in text or are represented in code (Level A).

- **1.3.2 Meaningful Sequence:** When the sequence in which content is presented affects its meaning, a correct reading sequence can be programmatically determined (Level A).

- **2.4.3 Focus Order:** If a web page can be navigated sequentially and the navigation sequences affect meaning or operation, focusable components receive focus in an order that preserves meaning and operability (Level A).

- **3.1.1 and 3.1.2 Language of Page/Parts:** The default human language of each web page (Level A) or of each passage or phrase in the content (Level AA) is defined in code.

- **4.1.1 Parsing:** The markup is written to standard specifications (Level A).

- **4.1.2 Name, Role, Value:** Interface elements are identified so that their name and role can be read by assistive technology and other user agents. There is a way for the program to set any values that users can set (Level A).

The full text of the WCAG 2.0 requirements can be found in Appendix B.

Summary

A solid structure depends on good coding practice. A site coded to standards, with all information written to be machine-readable, supports use of the site by different browsers or devices, including assistive technology.

- Pages are organized so that when code is read in the order it appears in the file, it not only makes sense, but it puts the most important information first.

- Stylesheets separate content from presentation, using code to communicate semantic meaning, such as content structure, emphasis, or function, as well as visual style.

- A site with solid structure does not create barriers in how it is constructed, so people can feel confident using it.

Mike Paciello has been a leader in promoting information and com-munication technology accessibility since the 1980s. He helped launch the Web Accessibility Initiative (WAI) and worked on both WAI and U.S. Section 508 standards.

He's also the founder and president of The Paciello Group (TPG), a consultancy working with software companies to make their prod-ucts accessible. We wanted to learn from Mike about the making of accessibility standards, and whether future iterations might be more "user-friendly."

An early commitment to people and technology.

From early in his career, Mike saw technology as a powerful enabler, and was compelled to make that potential available to everyone. "I feel an incredible obli-gation and responsibility to people—particularly, people with disabilities—and to technology."

Beginning to explore accessible electronic documents.

One of Mike's first projects was acting as the liaison between DEC and the National Braille Press, where he learned how much work it took to make documents acces-sible to the blind. To convert the DEC software manual to braille, people retyped the text into a "braille typewriter" of sorts, and the text was then printed. "It would take them a year to produce one book." The typical DEC documentation usually spanned several volumes and was regularly updated. "I asked, why not convert everything electronically? But they said there was no way to do that."

How to make large, complex documents usable and accessible generally, and spe-cifically, how to provide usability to blind and low vision users? Mike started to explore electronic document accessibility right around the birth of the web.

Markup languages bring meaning to electronic documents.

In the late 1980s and early 1990s Mike started working with SGML. "I thought, how about we use a markup language on an electronic document, and then a braille translator can read the markup language and produce braille?" He also realized that accessibility for blind and low vision users meant more than braille—that large text and listening to text were also commonly used, and a markup language had the potential of providing accessibility in those contexts as well.

At the first World Congress on Accessibility in 1991, Mike joined forces with col-leagues to create the International Committee for Accessible Document Design (ICADD). This group created the first international specification for accessible electronic documents, ICADD-22, which was to become an important contribution to the Web Content Accessibility Guidelines and accessibility elements in HTML.

profile continues on next page

A pioneer for web accessibility.

In 1995, Mike launched WebABLE, the first website dedicated to web accessibility for people with disabilities. When the Worldwide Web Consortium started up, Mike got involved, creating the accessibility pages for the W3C. He and other accessibility colleagues started an informal W3C working group called the *Web Accessibility Project,* focused on integrating accessibility into HTML. "The groundwork we started back then ultimately became what most people know as the first Web Content Accessibility Guidelines."

Even this early, Mike could see the lines blurring between the web and software and wanted to improve accessibility for both. "I was convinced that eventually everything on the desktop was going to move to the web—imagine that."

Eventually, Jim Miller and Tim Berners-Lee asked Mike to help create a more formal and extensive accessibility effort within the W3C. "The conversation went something like, 'We've been contacted by the federal government and asked to consider creating a formalized program in the W3C to deal with accessibility and disabilities. We would like you to do it. Are you interested?'"

Helping set standards for web accessibility.

In 2006, the Access Board asked Mike to co-chair an Advisory Committee to update U.S. federal accessibility regulations. He and Jim Tobias led the effort, which covered both Section 255, or the Disabled Persons' Telecommunications Access Act, and Section 508, accessibility for electronic and information technology. The committee was composed of representatives of 41 organizations, from disability groups and technology companies (including the Usability Professionals' Association), and included participants from Canada, Europe, Asia, and Australia.

Working on the new guidelines, "We turned it from a product-based standard into a characteristic-based standard, so it would be completely platform neutral." In addition, they broadened the guidelines to include themes from usability and interoperability, and to address cognitive disabilities. In April 2008, the group presented the new, improved Section 508 to the Access Board. Since 2013, the new rules are working their way through the federal rule-making process.

From Mike's perspective, the current process of creating technology and legal standards is flawed. "It takes years for the formalization and acceptance of standards." He advocates a rolling process, where elements can be added and changed more readily to keep the standards viable. But Mike is hopeful about the potential impact of the new Section 508. Awareness about accessibility is at an all-time high, as is government recognition of the need for accessibility standards. Mike predicts that once the Section 508 standards become law, they will be used as "the model for all other major government mandates worldwide."

CHAPTER 5

Easy Interaction: Everything Works

EZ Access on Amtrak Ticket Machine

Many people use these Amtrak ticketing machines and never notice the EZ Access options, but they are there for those who need them. Source: http://trace.wisc.edu/ez/

There's very little as fundamental to independence as being able to get around on your own, without needing assistance. For many people, getting around means using kiosks to purchase tickets. For trains, buses, subways ... touchscreen kiosks are everywhere. But how do you use one if you are blind?

Enter EZ Access, designed at the Trace Center. By adding tactile buttons and an audio interface, EZ Access makes touchscreens easy to operate for everyone, including people who can't see.

Even better, the EZ Access features are unobtrusive—they are available for those who need them, but do not get in the way of those who don't.

The ultimate design "fail" is a website or app that people can't get to work. By contrast, everyone loves sites that are easy to operate and whose interaction feels intuitive. They can use them successfully with any device or assistive technology, and the site makes them feel confident and capable.

One way to think of interaction failures is as "I can't" moments: "I can't figure out how to submit this form." "I can't select this menu item." "I can't figure out how to enter my phone number in the right format." As users, we want—and hope for—interfaces that are self-explanatory, guiding us as effortlessly as possible. The controls should be easy to understand and use, which leads to "I can" moments.

Creating websites and web applications that people can use might seem like a no-brainer, but it's not an easy task. With the myriad technologies that can be used for building, different devices and software for accessing, different modes of interaction, different user needs and preferences, it's a complex environment for creating sites and apps that don't break. And then there's the pace of change!

How Easy Interaction Supports Accessibility

In Chapter 4, "Solid Structure," we talked about the importance of producing websites and web applications that software, including assistive technology, can read. Now, we'll look at how people interact with websites, and what is needed for accessibility.

Interfaces can be difficult to operate using standard tools, never mind specialized technologies. For web accessibility, easy interaction must take into account different needs.

Lea

Don't make me work so hard.

I love my keyboard. I tried dozens until I found one that fits my hands perfectly, so I hardly have to move to type. Maybe you think I'm a bit over the top, but it makes a difference for me by the end of the day. Using a mouse takes more energy than you think, and I have to conserve mine if I'm going to make it through the day. So do me a favor and let me use my keyboard for everything. OK?

With easy interaction, people can use the product across all modes of interaction and operating with a broad range of devices.

- **Sites don't create barriers, or sites make barriers easy to overcome.** The worst barriers keep someone from using a site at all. A few years ago, there was a debate about whether interactive worlds like *Second Life* were accessible. Many people with disabilities used them, both for the general enjoyment and because the interactive environment made their disability invisible. Even for blind users, it turned out that the most inaccessible part of the interface—the one that kept them from using *Second Life* at all—was the sign-in screen! (*Second Life* has since fixed this problem, marking up the sign-in form correctly.) Even small barriers can drive a user away. These are the sites that "sort of work" if you can just figure out how to get around the speed bumps of things like confusing markup or navigation. As Clayton Lewis put it, "Many barriers to cognitive *accessibility* are the same as *usability* problems for a general user audience ... *but more severe.*"

- **Designs work for people.** When things work well, we hardly notice them. That's why bad designs are so annoying and frustrating. CAPTCHA[1] is an example of a perfect storm of bad interaction— hard for everyone to use, not just people with disabilities. CAPTCHAs try to make sure that a real person (rather than software) is filling out a form, so they display a code word in distorted letters. The idea is that robots or other software can't read the letters, even using character recognition. To make them accessible, CAPTCHAs can include a distorted audio version that is also supposed to be undecipherable by software. Unfortunately, both the visual and audio distortions are difficult for many people, even with good eyesight or hearing. People may have difficulty separating sounds from background noise or spelling words with difficult letter combinations. Ironically, CAPTCHAs aren't even very effective— a spammer can pay for keys to break them for under a penny each.

- **People can choose their own way to interact with a site.** Some disabilities impact dexterity, making it difficult to respond quickly or to operate some kinds of controls. For example, some people work best with tactile controls—buttons and other controls they can feel— while others work best with pointing devices. All of this adds up to

---

1 CAPTCHA stands for Completely Automated Public Turing test to Tell Computers and Humans Apart, but they can be so frustrating that Jared Smith from WebAIM suggests it should mean Completely Automated Patience Test to Confuse the Hell out of your Audience.

giving people the ability and means to control their own environment, the time and space to work at their own pace in their own way, and the software and hardware that works best for them.

Designing for Easy Interaction

Success in interaction design is largely a matter of following established patterns, so people can apply what they already know to new contexts. Using known and well-established interactive controls goes a long way in designing for easy interaction. There are specific considerations that will help make controls more usable for people using assistive technologies. And there are design considerations that make interaction more usable and enjoyable for everyone, including people with disabilities.

Identify and describe interactive elements

Interactive elements should be easy to distinguish from other elements on the page. For example, links and buttons can be identified in the following ways:

- **Visually.** Links are often colored and underlined, and buttons are identifiable by shape.
- **In code.** Link and button markup codes distinguish these elements, making it possible for browsers to identify them.
- **Through interaction.** Links and buttons can show their state, such as when they are active, through changes in their appearance. They can also be accessed through the keyboard or in lists of interactive elements constructed by assistive technology.

Between HTML, WAI-ARIA, and features of the technology platform, there are many options for providing accessible interactivity by using code to identify and describe interactive elements.

Use basic HTML codes correctly

In addition to coding interactive components, you can also describe their function programmatically. HTML has codes that help software communicate information about components to users.

With basic HTML, interaction is limited to links and form controls. The codes you use to provide interaction include the attributes needed to make the elements accessible. Implementing those elements fully, according to specification, goes far in providing accessible interactivity. Take, for example, a label for a text input field, as shown in Figure 5.1.

Visually, the label is related by proximity, usually appearing right before the field. In code, the label is related using the `<label for>` element and attribute, which programmatically connects the label with the input field. That way software can tell the user which type of information to enter into the field.

FIGURE 5.1
Labels are visually associated by proximity with text input fields. In code, labels are programmatically connected using the `<label>` element, the "for" attribute, and the input field's "id" attribute making the connection.

```
<label for="firstname">First name:</label>

<input type="text" id="firstname" />

<label for="lastname">Last name:</label>

<input type="text" id="lastname" />
```

Use WAI-ARIA for complex elements

Until recently, there was not the same built-in accessible support for complex, page-level interaction as there is for links and forms. But that is finally changing. With WAI-ARIA, you can identify and describe interactive elements in a way that software can read, so it is accessible to users of assistive technology.

For example, one interaction pattern is the "accordion" widget, which is a link that, when clicked, expands to show hidden content (see Figure 5.2). Clicking a second time collapses the content back to its hidden state. This pattern is helpful for content that may not be relevant to all users. It saves precious screen real estate, and also provides a way to learn more in context, without jumping to different pages or scrolling through one long page.

ARIA provides codes you can use to identify and describe interactive components like an accordion widget programmatically so that assistive technology can communicate information about the component to users. For example, in the case of an accordion widget, the "aria-expanded" attribute can be set programmatically to "true" or "false," depending on the state of the component.

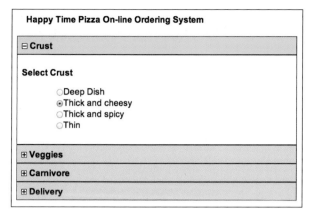

FIGURE 5.2
The OpenAjax
Alliance (www.oaa-accessibility.org)
provides examples and
downloadable code for
many common design
patterns, including an
accessible accordion
widget. (www.oaa-accessibility.org/
examplep/accordian1/)

ARIA is helpful for other interactions as well. For example, in the sample sign-up form, shown in Figure 5.3, error messages are coded with the attribute role="alert" so that the helpful in-line error messages can be announced to screen reader users.

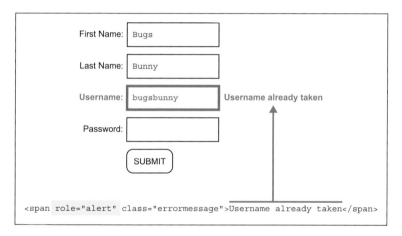

FIGURE 5.3
In this sample account sign-up form, alerts are identified programmatically using the ARIA role attribute.

Use features of the technology platform

When you are coding elements using programming other than HTML, you should use the features of the technology to fully identify and describe interactive elements. For the most part, technologies like Flash and Java have the necessary hooks for accessibility. Those who develop

The websites for financial service companies often include complex financial information, including real-time data, price charts, and information to help investors manage their money. The guidelines below are excerpted from Ann Chadwick-Dias and Marguerite Bergel's work with product development teams to make sure that their applications are accessible, especially for older customers managing their retirement funds.

1. Clearly indicate and manage focus.
   - Ensure users can visually track their focus when keyboard navigating.
   - Shift focus into layers as they open; return focus to the originating link once closed.
   - Keep users' focus on controls as they operate them (expand/collapse toggle).

2. Help users know where to begin and reinforce where they are.
   - Use style changes for selected menu items, buttons, and visited links in content pages.
   - Add a button that simulates the browser's Back button, if needed.
   - Mirror the page's information hierarchy in the code using proper semantic markup.

3. Clearly indicate what is interactive and *how* to interact with it.
   - Offer clear instructions or demos, where appropriate.
   - Change cursors and styles for interactive controls on hover.
   - Use active terminology on interactive elements.
   - Use ARIA to communicate custom controls' role and state to assistive technologies.

using these tools just need to use them correctly and to design so it is possible to code the interaction accessibly.

But you should consider the ramifications carefully before moving away from standard technologies. Is the interaction necessary to the purpose and goals of the product? If so, can you accomplish what's needed using standard coding? Exhaust the possibility of using standard web technologies before you make a commitment to a non-standard, and therefore less stable and accessible format.

Provide accessible instructions and feedback

In Chapter 4, *Organize code for clarity and flow*, we discussed how some modes of interaction rely on linearized access, and the code order

4. Progressively reveal content.

- Draw attention to changes (fading colored backgrounds, data loading indicators).
- Change content downstream of users' focus.
- Use ARIA live regions to announce updated content to assistive technologies.

5. Design forgiving controls and inputs.

- Use large click, grab, tap, drop targets. Wrap supporting icons in adjacent text links.
- Don't make controls too sensitive, requiring fine motor control.
- Add redundant text entry fields next to sliders.

6. Let users control movement on the page.

- Don't auto-play A/V content or loop animations users can't control.
- Warn users in advance if links launch A/V content.

7. Respect users' settings.

- Make fonts responsive to browsers' text size controls (e.g., IE's View>Text Size).
- Ensure that content wraps and containers adjust as font sizes scale.
- Don't override color display settings users set in their browser or operating system.

matters because it affects the order in which elements are presented. For example, the audio mode of a screen reader cannot present more than one piece of information or interactive option at a time. Interactive elements that are not sequenced correctly can create barriers for everyone, but especially for people relying on a linear presentation.

It's not the details of the interaction itself that create the barrier, but how it is structured in the code and presented to users. A simple rule of thumb is to design the page so that any changes made after it loads the first time happen "downstream" of the cursor.

The location in the code makes a real difference to the accessibility of forms and error messages. For example, as a user fills in a form, the code checks each entry to be sure it is valid. It might check to see if a username is available. But, if feedback is displayed *above* the field, the assistive technology doesn't see the change, and it simply proceeds to the next field. Even worse, some forms display error messages in a "modal" pop-up window that requires the user to close the window before correcting the errors. With the error messages no longer displayed, the user must try to remember the list of problems while looking for the fields to correct.

Or it could be that, after a user submits a form, software on the server identifies a problem with the submitted data and redisplays the form so the errors can be corrected. In some cases, the program positions the cursor in the field in question. Unfortunately, the error message is displayed at the top of the page. Not only will assistive technology not see this message, but most users won't see it either.

So as you are designing forms, you should make sure that any interactive feedback appears both in the code and on-screen in a way that makes sense when linearized. Most often, this means putting the inserted feedback after the element, so it is the next thing in the tab and reading order, as well as marking it with an ARIA role, as shown in the sample sign-up form in Figure 5.3.

Sequencing also matters for instructions. Sometimes, forms are coded so that instructions and labels appear after the form fields and buttons. Users (and assistive technology) have to read ahead to determine the purpose of each field and then backtrack to fill in the field. Be sure that the elements in a form follow a logical sequence: identify and describe an element before the interaction, both visually and in the code.

Instructions and labels that appear inside the field are problematic because they disappear when the field is activated. Users who need to look at the keyboard as they type will miss the hint entirely. Others won't remember the details in the instructions and labels once they are no longer displayed.

Carol

I don't understand what the screen is saying.

I love seeing photos of my grandchildren, particularly since they live so far away. My granddaughter set up a place where she can put up pictures and notes for me. I was excited, but it took me three tries and a phone call to get me connected. I thought I filled in all the answers correctly, but the same questions kept appearing. I'm sure that program was trying to tell me what to do, but I just couldn't understand what the screen was saying.

Support keyboard interaction

The point-and-click interaction model popularized by the mouse is *not* universally usable. Nonvisual users cannot see to point the mouse. People with dexterity issues may find mouse operations awkward and cumbersome. Some alternative input devices work by activating keyboard commands instead. Also, some people find keyboard control easier, more comfortable, and more efficient than pointing.

Provide a logical tab order

In Chapter 4, we talked about how the code order affects linear access to web pages in *Organize code for clarity and flow*. Code order has a significant impact on keyboard navigation, especially when using the tab key to cycle through actionable elements (interactive controls like buttons and links) on the page. Tabbing is a common navigation approach for keyboard users, similar to how mouse users will look for and click on links and controls. Keyboard users will press the tab key repeatedly until arriving at the desired element and then press Enter to activate the control.

With standard web pages, tab order is based on the sequence of elements in the code order. Other formats use other methods—for example, Flash calculates tab order based on the location of elements on the screen. In either case, it's important to test tab order to make sure it follows a logical progression.

While it's possible to manually set tab order in code, the best approach is to sequence elements appropriately, so the natural tab order works in a logical and usable fashion.

Don't require point-and-click interaction

Supporting keyboard interaction doesn't mean that you can never use complex interactions like drag and drop. Just make sure that all interactions have an option that does not require pointing.

Here are some things to keep in mind when designing interactions:

- **Hover:** Some devices do not support hover, such as touchscreens— hover all you want over a touchscreen, and nothing is going to happen! Hover actions can also be annoying when they are triggered inadvertently, such as when a menu is displayed simply because the mouse pointer crossed it on the way to another part of the screen. Hovers can also be distracting to people with cognitive or attention disabilities.

When the Apple iPhone first came out, the disability community was dismayed: there were almost no tactile controls, making the phone impossible for the blind and people with dexterity disabilities to use. But today, Apple's touchscreen devices—iPad and iPhone—have gained a following in the blind community because the interface is now designed with voice and gesture input and a built-in screen reader, called *VoiceOver* (see Figure 5.4).

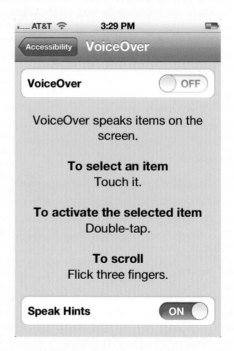

FIGURE 5.4
VoiceOver speaks what is tapped, and activates whatever item currently has focus on a double-tap.

With the success of VoiceOver, other companies are also building accessibility into their devices, although none have reached the level of VoiceOver. What's new, even revolutionary, about these features is that they are built into the platform operating systems, so they can be turned on and off without any special hardware or software.

When accessibility features get this easy, they start to become universal design. Both VoiceOver and Explore-by-Touch allow eyes-free use of the device for anyone whose eyes are otherwise occupied. Siri and other voice activation features are innovative uses of voice technology that let everyone interact with their devices easily.

- **Select:** Using "select" to trigger actions is problematic for keyboard users because events are activated inadvertently as soon as they are selected. The best approach is to use a select/activate model of interaction, where elements are selected and identified, and then explicitly activated by the user. Using this model, you can build one interaction mode that works universally.

- **Drag and drop:** This style of interaction makes direct manipulation of objects easy, but typically requires a pointing device and dexterity. Instead, you can offer a keyboard-accessible alternative way to move items from one place to another (see Figure 5.5).

FIGURE 5.5
This feature, collecting bookmarks for related items, requires a mouse to drag and drop items into the list. A simple Add button would make this more accessible.

Show which element has keyboard focus

Keyboard users also benefit from a clear indicator showing which element currently has focus. Browser software supplies a default focus indicator—typically a dotted outline around the element. However, keyboard usability can be improved by using CSS to provide stronger visual cues to help users make deliberate choices about which elements to interact with. Figure 5.6 shows an example of CSS code. Best practice is to provide the same visual cue as provided to indicate hover—for example, when the mouse or other pointing device is "hovering" over an element.

```
a:hover, a:active, a:focus { outline: 2px solid blue }
```

FIGURE 5.6
Use CSS to provide a visible outline around items that have keyboard focus. In this example, the same 2 pixel blue outline identifies which item is moused over (hover), active, or has keyboard focus.

We all love our smartphones, but how can someone who can't see dial the phone on a touchscreen?

The answer is the Talking Dialer, a free Android app from the Eyes-Free project (including T.V. Raman from Google). It cleverly redefines the interaction from the perspective of the user, rather than the device. Here's how it works (see Figure 5.7):

- Just touch the screen anywhere: that's where the "5" button is.

- Slide your finger up, down, left, right or diagonally to reach another number, based on the layout of a phone keypad.

- Talking Dialer announces the number.

When you have entered the whole phone number, tap anywhere at the bottom of the screen to start the call.

FIGURE 5.7
Starting from where your finger touches the screen, sliding it in any direction selects a number. For example, go to the left for a "4" or up diagonally to the right for a "3."

Don't trap keyboard focus

"Keyboard trap" can happen with embedded objects, such as videos, applets, and Flash. When the focus is trapped, users can't get in or out of an element without a pointing device, like a mouse. Techniques for avoiding keyboard trap are dependent in large part on the technology of the embedded object. Ideally, entering and exiting an embedded object uses the same navigation methods as a web page—namely, tabbing and arrow keys. For technologies that do not support standard navigation, provide a keyboard option and document it so that keyboard users can avoid getting trapped.

Make controls large enough to operate easily

Controls on-screen may not be three dimensional, but users still need dexterity to operate them. Physical issues from arthritis to tremors can make it hard to accurately use a control, but so can context like working on a crowded airplane without enough elbow room, or even wearing

Glenn's sister had a problem. She loved to read, but her cerebral palsy made handling both books and most ebook readers hard for her. Luckily, Glenn is an engineer with the skills to take on projects to make her life easier.

They found a children's book reader that she could use, but it didn't come with books she was interested in. The Kindle was a good start because it had buttons instead of a touchscreen, but the buttons were too small and stiff for her.

A little bit of homebrew electronics later, Glenn created the Frankenkindle, substituting a set of large buttons for the ones that come with the Kindle (see Figure 5.8).

FIGURE 5.8
DIY assistive technology for the Kindle.
http://breadboardconfessions.blogspot.
com/2011/08/frankenkindle-prototype-
demo.html

gloves. People navigating the web using a touchscreen mobile device can run into difficulty trying to, for example, select one of a set of radio buttons, or click a submit button. Even responsive sites may not take into account the differences in size between a pointing device and a fingertip.

The following guidelines help make controls easy to use:

- **Minimize the fine-motor skills needed for interactive elements.** Make buttons and touch points large enough.

- **Space controls.** Put enough space between controls so that users don't accidentally activate the wrong one.

- **Minimize the complexity of the action required.** Choose controls that do not require timing or managing multiple actions when possible. Watch out for controls like multi-level menus that require a steady hand to operate.

Let users control the operation of the interface

Try to avoid making changes that are not triggered by an explicit user request. For example, the "carousel" of highlighted stories on a home page typically advances automatically, based on an estimation of time needed to get through the content. Uncontrolled motion in an interface is distracting and impacts comprehension. Some users need more time to take in the information, so at a minimum, provide a way to stop the action. (See Chapter 9, "Accessible Media" for more information about multimedia.)

A better approach is to load the first image and provide clear controls for advancing through the stories. This applies to all moving elements, including media such as video and audio. Don't play media automatically. Instead, wait for users to elect to play the media. Autoplay is not only distracting, but can also cause problems for people in a quiet setting or using a low-bandwidth connection to the web (such as a weak mobile phone signal).

Another common practice is opening links in a new window, usually with the rationale that it will help users return to the originating website because they can just close the window. Unfortunately, opening a new window starts a new browsing history. When users navigate in this new window and try to use the back button to return to the first website, they can't do so because the first website is not in the history for the programmatically opened window. Indeed, this practice could end up having the exact opposite of the desired effect—in that, users will not be able to find their way back.

Deciding whether to open a new window is a simple illustration of an important principle: **Don't take actions on behalf of users that they can already accomplish on their own.**

People who like to open links in new windows can achieve this experience on their own, using built-in browser controls. People who do not like opening links in a new window cannot *not* use that behavior if you program it into the interface. As designers, we need to respect the boundaries of the user environment.

Design for contingencies

Like the fire protection and emergency exit systems of a building, digital products must also be built so that when something does go wrong, harmful effects are minimized or prevented through error response and recovery.

Defensive Design

37signals defines defensive design as "design for when things go wrong." In their book, *Defensive Design for the Web*, they define four ways defensive design supports users and helps them recover:

- **Validates** data to check for mistakes before they frustrate the user.
- **Expands** available options based on the user's implied intent.
- **Protects** site visitors from server errors and broken links with informative messages.
- **Assists** the user before mistakes happen.

Errors can occur on many levels. Some, like broken links or programming glitches, are a matter of writing valid code (see Chapter 4, *Code to standards*). Others occur because of confusion about how things work, or through simple mistakes, like clicking on the wrong menu item when your elbow is jostled, or poking a small screen. There is no such thing as a fail-safe system. No interface is intuitive to every user, and no user is on target every time.

Designing for contingencies is about using design to minimize the impact of errors and system failures when they can't be avoided.

For example, you should support users who are submitting information, ordering a product, or posting a comment.

- **Provide a review page.** Allow users to review their input before submitting.
- **Give options for editing the submission.** Support an iterative review/edit process to give users plenty of time and opportunity to be certain about their submission.
- **Provide a confirmation page.** When the information is submitted, confirm the transaction and provide instructions about making any additional changes. Confirmation pages not only provide a nice ending to the interaction, but they also work as conversation:

  User: I'd like to place an order. Here's all my information.

  Your site: Thanks. Got it. We'll send this to you within three days.

Good communication can also make the system easier to operate and to avoid errors. For example, if the system requires a specific date format, provide an example date right before the input field.

If an error does occur, provide helpful and accessible feedback in response to input errors. The feedback should appear with the element containing the error, and should provide clear instructions for how to correct the input, as shown in the sample sign-up form in Figure 5.3.

Allow users to request more time

Time is a challenge for many people. It may take more time for someone using assistive technologies, such as a screen reader, text enlarger, or alternative input device like a joystick. They may read more slowly or need more time to think about what they are reading. Other people need time to simply move their muscles, and it may take a long time to get their arm and hand to coordinate to interact with a link, button, or field. Time-outs can ruin their experience.

Some websites have features that are triggered by time—a common example is the timeout feature used for security reasons by many web applications. When a user logs into the system, the system notes the time and watches the activity. If a predetermined time passes with no activity from the user, the system times out and logs the user off.

A well-designed timeout process alerts users prior to logging them off, and provides them with the option to continue the session. Also, if the system ends up indeed logging off the user, it caches whatever activity they had initiated in the browser. This allows the user to log back in and pick up where they left off.

Who Is Responsible for Easy Interaction?

Design and development collaborate on easy interaction. It is possible to create interactions that are both innovative and accessible, but it takes coordination. Working together to come up with ideas and ways of coding the design can take experimentation, prototyping, and cleverness in solving problems.

When the design team understands what's possible within the constraints of the medium, and the developers understand what's required for universally usable interaction, the results are more likely to be accessible for everyone.

WCAG 2.0 and Easy Interaction

The guidelines for Easy Interaction map to the following WCAG 2.0 requirements.

A site with easy interaction is **Operable**, coded to support a variety of interactions, such as a mouse, keyboard or assistive technology. It also ensures that users can both **Perceive** and **Understand** how to interact with the site.

A site with easy interaction meets the guidelines:

- **2.1 Keyboard Accessible:** Make all functionality available from a keyboard (Guideline).
- **3.2 Predictable:** Make web pages appear and operate in predictable ways (Guideline).
- **3.3 Input Assistance:** Help users avoid and correct mistakes (Guideline).

The requirements for easy interaction are:

- **1.3.2 Meaningful Sequence:** Programs can determine the correct order of the content (Level A).
- **2.1.1 and 2.1.3 Keyboard:** All functionality can be operated through the keyboard without requiring specific timing for each keystroke with no exceptions (Level AAA) or except where the underlying function requires input that depends on the path of the user's movement and not just the endpoints (Level A).
- **2.1.2 No Keyboard Trap:** The keyboard focus does not get "trapped" in a component (Level A).
- **2.4.3 Focus Order:** Elements on the page receive focus in a meaningful order (Level A).
- **2.4.7 Focus Visible:** Any keyboard operable user interface has a mode of operation where the keyboard focus indicator is visible (Level AA).
- **3.2.1 On Focus:** The context does not change based only on a component receiving focus (Level A).
- **3.2.2 On Input:** The context does not change when a setting is changed, unless the user has been advised of the behavior before using the component (Level A).
- **3.2.5 Change on Request:** Changes of context are initiated only by user request or a mechanism is available to turn off such changes (Level AAA).

- **3.3.1 Error Identification and 3.3.3 Error Suggestions:** An item with an error is identified and the error is described to the user in text (Level A) and with a suggestion (Level AA) when possible.

- **3.3.2 Labels or Instructions:** Labels or instructions are provided when content requires user input (Level A).

- **3.3.4 and 3.3.6 Error Prevention:** Actions that submit information are reversible and checked for all (Level AAA) or for legal and financial transactions (Level AA).

- **3.3.5 Help:** Context-sensitive help is available (Level AAA).

- **4.1.2 Name, Role, Value:** Interface elements are identified so that their name and role can be read by assistive technology and other user agents. There is a way for the program to set any values that users can set (Level A).

The full text of the WCAG 2.0 requirements can be found in Appendix B.

Summary

Making the interaction easy for people with disabilities is an extension of making interaction easy for everyone. Interactive elements are identified clearly and are designed to be easy to use.

The site supports interaction with a keyboard, allowing assistive technology to emulate the keyboard. This also requires that the keyboard tab order make sense, matching the visual presentation.

A site with easy interaction enables users to control the interface, with large enough controls. It avoids taking unexpected actions for users that they can do on their own. Easy interaction also includes both preventing and handling errors in an accessible way.

Derek Featherstone is founder and lead of Simply Accessible, a consultancy that works to bring accessibility into organizations through consulting, training, workshops, and support. Derek is a well-known and well-respected advocate for accessible user experience, moving beyond technical accessibility to support good and successful experiences for everyone. Interactivity is a complex challenge for accessibility, making sure that sites and apps are operable in different ways on different devices. We wanted to learn from Derek how best to approach a moving target like accessible interaction.

People are the starting point.

Concern for people is the primary driver for Derek and his colleagues at Simply Accessible. "It has to be about the people who are actually using the site or application to accomplish something. If it's not about them, then what's the point?"

Best accessibility techniques are constantly changing.

Derek's team works from a knowledge base of accessible techniques, built over years of user research and usability testing. From there, they use observation and experimentation to come up with better techniques for coding, designing, and writing content that improves the user experience.

Technical remediation can help make interaction accessible.

Most often, Derek's team is called on to make an existing website or app accessible. Often, the designs are visually rich and appealing, and convey information and relationships among elements in a visual way. However, those visual details are not always in the code.

For example, many social media sharing badges don't have alt text that accurately reflects the contents of the badge. Visually, you can tell whether an item has been liked or shared, but the code doesn't contain the same information. Derek and his colleagues have been working on a script that would make state and status information available in the code where it's available to assistive technology.

We know it would be better if these elements were natively accessible. We also know that change doesn't happen right away. We keep our fixes on file so we can use them while the people in charge of social sharing badges work on making them more accessible.

"Our entire team views accessibility as part of overall user experience and not as a separate thing that needs to be done afterwards." However, in practice, clients often come to accessibility late in the process, when there is little hope of changing the course of the design to produce a more accessible outcome. "What we usually do is say, given what you've designed, here's what you need to do to make it work in a more accessible way."

profile continues on next page

Integrated accessibility produces the best outcomes.

But in some projects, they are brought in early and remain part of the team throughout the project. These projects are the most successful. "What it comes down to is having people switched on right from the beginning of the project. They understand accessibility as more than a technical checklist." With an early commitment, accessibility becomes part of the well-established user experience practice. "One of the most important things to achieve success is to have all accessibility touch points built into the process right from the beginning."

Tools help teams integrate accessible components.

Derek and his colleagues have had good success providing teams with tools that make it easier to build accessible products. One tool is an accessibility guide, integrated into the organizational style guide or branding guide. Another is a code repository and pattern library containing elements like modal dialogs or tool tips that can be easily dropped into code. "One of our goals is to eliminate excuses. We think about all the different pressures people feel when building a site and try to address them."

The most influential tool for accessibility is clear purpose.

In cases where Derek has been able to influence design, the best tool in guiding an accessible process has been clear purpose. "Asking the original question, what is the purpose of this page and what are we trying to help people do. And once we get answers, we can start asking questions like, how does somebody who uses voice recognition software because they don't have the ability to use their hands, how are they going to activate that particular type of control?"

Solutions come from different places.

Derek tells a story of a woman who needed a very specific design approach for accessible interaction. She was a quadriplegic, but had enough strength in one arm to lift her hand and operate a large touchscreen. Her greatest challenges were radio buttons and checkboxes, which were too small for her to activate accurately. Derek created a stylesheet she could install in her browser that would resize radio buttons and checkboxes ten times the size they normally appeared.

The story illustrates that accessible interaction isn't about finding the one solution that works for everyone. "We can create one solution that works for most people's abilities, but there are some people that need accommodation for their disabilities that a designer or developer can't take into account in their work." In these cases, the work of the designer and developer is to make the design flexible and adaptable. That way, browsers and assistive technology can take elements of the design and adapt them to meet the specific needs of the user.

CHAPTER 6

Helpful Wayfinding: Guides Users

Getting Around an Airport

Paul Mijkensanaar designed the wayfinding system for 10 international airports. This photo is from the bilingual wayfinding system at the Geneva International Airport. (www.mijksenaar.com)

In the physical world, we rely on maps, street signs, and how spaces are designed to help us get around. A corridor looks different than a meeting room, and we know one is for passage and the other is for gathering and discussion. Signs identify the routes and destinations, helping us get from here to there.

When signage uses consistent colors, typography, and icons and is placed in a visible location, it can be easy for people to find their way, even around a crowded airport.

In both the online and physical world, people rely on familiar patterns to help them find their way more easily. A mix of conventions and experience helps everyone locate cues in either the physical environment or an online interface, using the design of directional signs or interaction features like menus, buttons, and links. When these features are easily found where they are most expected, it takes less effort to use them. Table 6.1 compares the tools for wayfinding in the online and real worlds.

Wayfinding and orientation are especially important on the web where users have a relatively small window into the site (and an even smaller view on the tiny screens of mobile devices). Every site needs orientation features to help users know where they are, and it needs wayfinding features to help users find their way to the information or function they came to the site for. When these features anticipate users' needs, it makes using a site easier for everyone.

TABLE 6.1 WAYFINDING IN THE REAL WORLD AND ONLINE

Wayfinding in the Real World	Wayfinding Online
Architectural features define the space with paths, doorways, and so on.	Semantic features define the space with areas for information, interaction, orientation, and navigation.
Conventions for the placement of signs help people find them easily. There are often local standards, but they may vary.	Conventions for the placement of types of links or features help people find them easily, but there are no global standards.
Visually distinct landmarks help keep people oriented. (For example, "Let's meet at the clock at the station.")	Visual design, the types of content, and presentation details vary by the type of page, and help people stay oriented as they move around the web.
Signs mark places (shop signs, street signs).	Headings, landmarks, and visual cues mark places.
Signs point out paths to other destinations.	Menus and links point out paths to other destinations.
Signs have colors, shapes, and symbols to go along with the words.	Colors, icons, and typography go along with words to provide multiple cues.
Directories are organized in a logical order (alphabetical, by type, or by location).	Menus and page elements are organized in a logical order.
Space maps provide an overview.	Site maps provide an overview.

Trevor

When I can learn the pattern, I can find my way.

I like games. The ones where you have to find your way around a maze are good because I can go over them, and I can learn how they work. It's OK to get lost and have to figure out a game.

But when I'm trying to find something, like an assignment for school, I don't like getting lost. I want to know where I'm going—because it's easier, and it's easier to find things again when I need them. When it's clear and I can tell where I am, I like the site. It's like learning how to walk to school on my own. I practiced finding my landmarks, so I would know where to turn. I know that it's 500 steps from 1st Avenue to the first street I have to cross. Just like I know what to click on to get to my history class page on my school's website.

How Helpful Wayfinding Supports Accessibility

Wayfinding includes both navigation (features that let users move around the site) and orientation (identifying the current location). A site with wayfinding that works well for both visual navigation and all kinds of assistive technology makes the online environment usable for everyone.

With helpful wayfinding, **people can navigate a site, feature, or page following self-explanatory signposts.**

- **Navigation options make sense.** It can take more effort to navigate a website or web application using assistive technology, which makes every action more important. Links that aren't clear and menus that are confusing can result in ping-ponging among sections and back-tracking. Clear wayfinding reduces the chance of making the wrong choice among navigation options.

- **The interface supports exploration.** No one wants to be pushed through a chute with no options. Sometimes the fun is in finding your own way through a site. When a site has good wayfinding, exploration is safe, because it offers clear cues about where each link or menu option leads, and it has consistent ways back.

- **People know where they are.** We all like to know where we are. When people are following a link or diving into the middle of a site, they need to know where they have landed, and what's available on this page. A site designed for easy wayfinding provides strong orientation cues so that everyone can use them, no matter how they are accessing the site.

How to Design Helpful Wayfinding

People rarely go online for the sheer joy of navigating around a site or app. (Perhaps people working on user experience do, but it's not the most usual reason.) The goal in designing navigation is to make it so intuitive that it becomes invisible to the user. With well-designed wayfinding, users can find their way around with minimal effort.

Create consistent cues for orientation and navigation

People tend to navigate partly by using the cues they experience in real time and partly by using a cognitive map, or mental construct, of the space (real or digital) they are navigating. Even small variations can be disorienting.

Although a clear and consistent model is important for any user, it is especially important for people who use screen readers and other technologies that read the page linearly. For linear access, consistent placement of elements and use of consistent semantic markup, including headings, helps users form mental models.

A visual user, for example, might quickly learn that there is a logo in a banner at the top of the page, search in the upper-right corner, and see a colorful title marking the beginning of the main content. A nonvisual user might equally quickly learn that the same title is the second heading on the page and use that model to jump rapidly to content on other pages.

Present things that are the same in the same way

One way to help users find their way around a site is to be consistent in how elements of the site are presented and labeled, which doesn't mean that the site must be boring with no variation or texture. However, elements of the site that form important landmarks should be consistent:

- Describe or label the same thing in the same way each time.
- Be consistent about the location in the page structure of key navigational elements, including menus and links to features like contact pages.

Research with older adults found some distinctly different patterns in how they interacted with websites.

- They were "cautious clickers" who spent more time reading before deciding to click on a link.
- They were more likely to try to click on text that was not linked, hoping that it would let them find the information they wanted.
- They had more difficulty understanding where they were within a site. For example, they would click on the current page link in the left menu.

When the team redesigned pages to accommodate their needs, older adults had less trouble navigating. Their design recommendations were:

- Use action words as links.
- Present links in an obvious and consistent way.
- Include images used as icons or bullets in the link.
- Use simple, clear navigational cues and labels.
- Use secondary or pop-up windows rarely.

"Web Usability and Age: How Design Changes Can Improve Performance" by Ann Chadwick-Dias, Michelle McNulty, and Tom Tullis. **http://dl.acm.org/citation. cfm?id=957212**

The relationship between links and the pages they point to should also be consistent. Consider these basic rules:

- The text of the link should accurately communicate the page or feature that the link connects to.
- The text of the link and the title of the target page should be similar, if not identical.

Differentiate things that are different

When navigating in the real world, differences help you stay oriented. You recognize the corner where you turn not just by the name of the road, but because you recognize the building on the corner, or because the traffic on the main road sounds different than the quiet side streets.

It's the same on websites. Differences in layout and page elements help identify the page type or site section. For example, when encountering a carousel of big images and bold headlines, you might assume that you are on a home page. A page that is mostly information is probably a content page. And a page with a lot of links is for navigation, or what Ginny Redish calls a "pathway" page.

There can be too much consistency if it blurs important distinctions. People like predictability, so when the same words, images, or buttons do different things, it's disorienting and breaks their mental models.

Provide orientation cues

Orientation—knowing where you are—is an important part of successful wayfinding. When arriving at a page, how easily can you tell where you are and answer questions like "What is on this page?" or "What site is this page part of?" and "Where am I in this site?"

Orientation is important whether the journey starts from the home page or the user has landed in the middle of a site by following a link. In fact, users are more likely to start from the middle of a site than to navigate from the home page. Either way, the site needs clear "You Are Here" orientation cues, integrated into the design, content, and code.

- **Identify the site.** Be sure that it's easy to find the name of the site and to identify the organization behind the site.

- **Title the page.** The page title is the text that appears in the title bar of the browser. It's also the text that displays in a bookmarks list, in search results, and it is the first thing announced by screen reader software. The title tells what the page is about, and it also provides orientation cues. A good convention is to include page title, section name, and site name (in that order) in the <title> tag.

- **Provide good headings.** Headings describe the main topic of the page, as well as sections of content. Marking up headings using the correct markup (<h1–h6>) makes it easier for people who use assistive technology to find them.

- **Start with an overview.** It's common for users to leave sites if they don't see what they are looking for quickly. "Bouncing" is part of general behavior on the web, but you can help people make an accurate assessment by providing good content overviews.

- **Highlight the current location.** There are many ways to identify where a page fits into a site, from the page title to highlighting the menu item for the section to breadcrumb navigation.

- **Use multiple cues.** Providing more than one cue for orientation helps both visual and verbal thinkers. For example, using an icon with color-coding and a strong text label provides three ways to identify a page or feature.

When describing the interface, avoid using details like color or even location on the screen as the only cues in the instructions. Directions like "in the upper-left corner" don't mean much to someone navigating by audio. It's okay to use color and location along with other nonvisual cues: "The blue link labeled 'Contact Us' in the upper-left corner."

Provide clear landmarks within the page

Once visitors have gotten to a page, they still need to find their way around. Good visual design cues, good headings and other labels, and good underlying structure have to work together to make this process easy for everyone. When they do, the parts of the page are easy to differentiate both visually and in the code so they are available to assistive technology.

One way to provide a navigation map of the page is to use links that jump to specific areas of the page. These are often called *skip links* because they let a site visitor skip over sections of the page to go directly to key locations on the page. This is especially important as a way to skip over repeated blocks of content, like the links and logos in the heading of the page (see Figure 6.1).

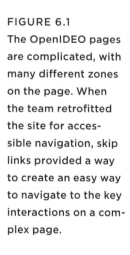

FIGURE 6.1
The OpenIDEO pages are complicated, with many different zones on the page. When the team retrofitted the site for accessible navigation, skip links provided a way to create an easy way to navigate to the key interactions on a complex page.

Lea

Links at the top of the page make navigation easier for me.

I like pages with links at the top of the page. It's really helpful on long pages with a lot of sections. I can figure out what's on the page without a lot of work. When I first saw a link to jump to the content, I didn't know what it was for, but it sure made navigating with a keyboard easier.

A better way to code navigation is with HTML5 elements and ARIA roles. These are complementary ways to identify parts of the page (see Table 6.2 and Figure 6.2). Adding elements and roles makes pages semantically rich by embedding information about the purpose of different elements. This information is then available for software—browsers, search engines, assistive technology—to use to enhance the user experience. For example, screen readers provide controls to move focus among the sections, which lessens the need for skip links as a way to bypass blocks of content. By coding boundaries around elements, you create clear landmarks that do not rely on visual properties, such as outlines or background color.

Because HTML is in a transitional phase, one of the challenges of working with these new standards is that using both elements and roles can create some duplication. For example, using both the ‹main› HTML element and the "main" ARIA role means that some screen readers will announce both, and users will hear, "main main." Over time, many of the ARIA roles will be incorporated into HTML5, and assistive technology

TABLE 6.2 HTML5 AND ARIA NAVIGATION

HTML5 Element	ARIA Role
‹article›	"article"
‹aside›	"complementary"
‹footer›	"contentinfo"
‹header›	"banner"
‹nav›	"navigation"
‹section›	"region"
‹main›	"main"
	"search"

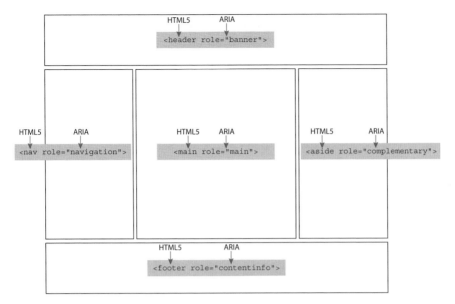

FIGURE 6.2
HTML5 elements and ARIA roles are complementary. Including both of them in your site provides a solid code structure and good navigation around the page.

will work with the standards in a more consistent way. Until then, using ARIA roles and HTML5 elements is the best approach to ensure that this important information is available to all users.

Provide alternative ways to navigate

It's important to reiterate: there is no *one way* to provide accessibility. The solution instead is to provide alternatives. For helpful wayfinding, this means offering different navigational options.

Most sites include more than one way to move around the site: menus, links, a sitemap, or search. Providing alternatives improves the chance that people will find what they are looking for.

For many people, given the choice of browsing through menus to explore options versus using search, search wins. For people with disabilities, for whom navigation can be slower and more difficult, search provides the means to jump directly to the right page. Many sites have realized the universal appeal of search and have made it prominent on the home page so it's easy to use to navigate.

You might not realize that the turn-by-turn text directions in Google Maps that so many people rely on started as an accessibility feature (see Figure 6.3).

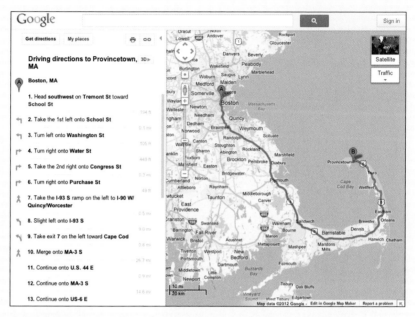

FIGURE 6.3

The original interface to Google Maps was entirely visual. Users would explore the map, including all the rich information about local features, and follow the guide on the visual map to get from place to place.

T.V. Raman, a research scientist at Google, created the first Textual Maps UI. As he wrote in his blog in 2006, "When using spoken output, this visual richness can get in the way of quickly listening to the results of a maps query."

His solution was an alternative interface that "serves up directions very efficiently when working with a screen reader or a braille display. ... It's extremely useful for blind and visually impaired users, as well as an effective solution for those times when you're at a nongraphical display and need to quickly look up a location. Just type a simple English query of the form start address to end address and quickly get the information you're looking for. Though we added this option to enhance the accessibility of Google Maps for blind and low-vision users, perhaps others will find this alternative view a useful addition to their maps arsenal."

You can read his blog entry from December 26, 2006: http://googleblog. blogspot.com/2006/12/speech-friendly-textual-directions.html

Who Is Responsible for Wayfinding?

Creating helpful wayfinding relies on both good design practices and user research. Understanding how your audience thinks about the information architecture is critical.

The design and content teams are responsible for strong information architecture, backed up by good user research. The teams should look for opportunities to help users make their way through the space and provide clear, distinctive landmarks to help them stay oriented.

In addition, it's important that wayfinding elements in the design and content are supported by the code, with landmarks that provide alternative ways to navigate a site or application.

WCAG 2.0 and Helpful Wayfinding

The guidelines for Helpful Wayfinding map to the following WCAG 2.0 requirements.

A site with helpful wayfinding is **Operable** and **Understandable**, with landmarks for orientation and wayfinding presented both in the content and code.

Wayfinding relies on being:

- **2.4 Navigable:** Provide ways to help users navigate, find content, and determine where they are (Guideline).
- **3.2 Predictable:** Make web pages appear and operate in predictable ways (Guideline).

The requirements for helpful wayfinding are:

- **2.4.1 Bypass Blocks:** Users can bypass blocks of repeated content (Level A).
- **2.4.2 Page Titled:** Web pages have titles that describe topic or purpose (Level A).
- **2.4.4 and 2.4.9 Link Purpose (In Context or Link Only):** The purpose of each link can be determined from the link text alone (Level AAA) or from the link text together with context (Level A).
- **2.4.5 Multiple Ways:** More than one way is available to locate a web page within a set of web pages, except for pages that are a step in a process (Level AA).

- **2.4.6 and 2.4.10 Headings and Labels:** Headings and labels describe topic or purpose (Level AA) and are used to organize content (Level AAA).

- **2.4.8 Location:** Information about the user's location within a set of web pages is available (Level AAA).

- **3.2.3 Consistent Navigation:** Navigational mechanisms that are repeated on a set of web pages are presented consistently (Level AA).

- **3.2.4 Consistent Identification:** Components that have the same functionality within a set of web pages are identified consistently (Level AA).

The full text of the WCAG 2.0 requirements can be found in Appendix B.

Summary

Helpful wayfinding depends on consistent, understandable cues that help users know where they are (orientation) and how to get where they want to go (navigation).

Some aspects of wayfinding are part of the content and presentation design: titles for pages, naming things that are the same in the same way each time (and differentiating things that are different), and including information about where users are in a page, site, or process.

Helpful wayfinding also relies on cues in the code, including ARIA landmarks, which act as descriptive landmarks for navigating around the page, and descriptive coding for navigation elements.

Steve Faulkner has been an accessibility engineer since 2001, first with Vision Australia and currently with The Paciello Group. He has a hand in developing HTML5 and WAI-ARIA specifications as a member of W3C working groups, and is editor of W3C specifications on HTML5, Using ARIA in HTML, accessibility APIs, and text alternatives. In short, Steve has accessibility chops.

Because much of what's needed is beneath the surface of a page, we asked Steve to explain what user experience designers should know about how code supports accessibility.

Elements of an accessible user interface.

Web accessibility is largely about providing the information needed to make a user interface accessible to assistive technology (AT). This is accomplished via an accessibility application programming interface (API)—a standardized way of specifying elements of an interface. For accessibility, Steve explains, "One piece of the puzzle is for information to be defined by an accessibility API. The second piece of the puzzle is for AT to make use of it."

For the web, every HTML element has a role, states, and properties that are defined in the technology specification—"what it is, what it does, and where it's at, at this point in time." That information is expressed by the accessibility API in the browser so that assistive technology can make use of it. "For example, with a heading, one of the properties might be its level, and whether it's editable, visible, or linked." Information in the accessibility API allows assistive technology to, for example, create a list of headings or move keyboard focus to the main heading of a page.

An accessibility API needs more than HTML.

There are gaps in how native HTML elements support the accessibility API. "Some decisions about what goes into HTML and what doesn't don't take into account accessibility requirements." For example, the role "main" is not represented in the HTML5 specification as an element, despite the expressed need for AT users to move cursor focus to the main content area. Other roles are defined, such as header, footer, and navigation: "I guess the thinking was, anything that's not something else must be the main content."

Also, HTML elements are not always used correctly. As an example, Steve explained that HTML buttons have been part of the specification for 15 years. However, developers build custom buttons using elements like images and links that are coded to behave like buttons. Typically, this is because "They have to please whoever makes the design decisions. To achieve a certain visual effect across different browsers and platforms, they can't always use standard controls." In these cases, "WAI-ARIA is the only way to supplement the necessary information for assistive technologies."

WAI-ARIA fills the gaps.

WAI-ARIA fills out the accessibility API, enhancing the descriptive information contained in native HTML controls and back-filling information for elements that are used for other than their intended purpose.

For example, ARIA provides explicit roles and properties to assist in wayfinding for users of assistive technology. Like "stepping stones," ARIA landmark roles allow assistive technology users to step through the content of the page to find the content area of interest.

HTML5, ARIA, or both?

In general, support for ARIA is more robust than accessibility support for new HTML5 features, because it's been around longer and has benefited from successful collaborations between accessibility experts and software vendors. "I'm not saying that it's good across the board, mainly due to some AT vendors just putting their heads in the sand, which has the effect of doing a disservice to their users." And you can count on support for ARIA in the future. "As far as ARIA is concerned, it will remain relevant for many years to come. As new issues and technologies emerge, there will be new related updates to the ARIA specs to fill in any gaps."

It's best to think of ARIA as complementary to HTML. "A good rule of thumb is, when there's a native HTML structure, element, or attribute that's well supported, use it. If that's not enough, use the appropriate ARIA semantics."

Advice for project teams.

Steve encourages developers to add ARIA landmark roles. "The good thing about landmarks is that you can add them to your current code, and they don't have any design effects." For interactive widgets that provide complex interactions, he recommends looking to existing libraries, such as JQuery or Dojo—code with WAI-ARIA already built in.

But he also sees the need for a change in mindset in how we build websites and applications. Project efforts often focus on the business transactions that occur on the back end, with little thought given to the user interface. "You tend to find back-end coders developing front ends without understanding what makes a user interface usable, let alone accessible."

On the design end, Steve urges designers to understand that design elements are not just "pixels on a page," but rather semantic containers for information described in code. "I don't think designers need to know how to code. They do need to understand that there's a give and take between what can be done, given the requirement to actually code."

Overall, he believes project teams must include user interface expertise. "What's needed is the realization within a team of the value of having people who understand usable UI design and can bring it to fruition using the code."

CHAPTER 7

Clean Presentation: Supports Meaning

ClearRX Medication Labeling System

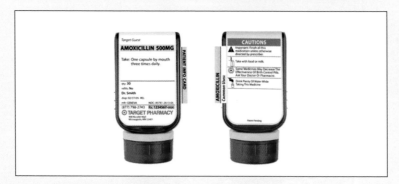

With ClearRX, the important information—drug name, dosage, instructions—takes precedence over secondary details, like manufacturer and pharmacy information. Precautions are detailed clearly and prominently on the other side of the bottle, using plain language and clarifying icons.

School of Visual Arts student Deborah Adler used her design training to improve packaging for medications in her Safe RX thesis project. She was inspired by her grandmother, who accidentally took her husband's medication because she was confused by the packaging.

Deborah identified the unclear elements in the current packaging and created prototypes with possible improvements. Target took Deborah's ideas and developed them further into the ClearRX system, which includes pill and liquid bottles and a measuring syringe. Clear presentation was a key area of improvement, modifying the design to enable easy identification and comprehension.

"Clean," "elegant," and "simple" are all words that describe the impact of a design with a clean visual presentation. By contrast, designs that are "cluttered," "busy," or "garish" don't seem as easy to understand and use.

An elegant visual presentation is the outcome of a straightforward, purposeful approach to visual and information design. Using techniques like white space, alignment, and emphasis, clean designs show relationships among elements and create an information hierarchy that tells the viewer what is related and what is important. Clarity in the presentation of elements in a design enhances both usability and accessibility.

When a site is also designed to be flexible, adapting gracefully to different ways of formatting the display, it is more accessible. It allows users to change the font size, simplify the layout, or hide distracting elements to be able to read the page. In today's web, designing for flexibility also makes it easy for a site to be responsive to different screen sizes, from the smallest smartphone to giant desktop monitors.

How Clean Presentation Supports Accessibility

A clean, clear visual design helps everyone make sense of the information and functionality of a website or web application. Cluttered or complex pages are difficult for everyone to use effectively, but pose extra challenges for people with disabilities. For example, people who use assistive technology, such as enlarged browser displays or screen magnification software, only have access to a small viewport at any one time. Some cognitive disabilities affect concentration and attention, making distractions even more disruptive. As we'll discuss in Chapter 9, "Accessible Media," animated or flashing elements can even cause physical harm.

With clean presentation, **people can perceive and understand elements in the design.**

- **Pages adapt to different display requirements.** An accessible website or app allows users to modify the display. For example, people with low vision use software that can enlarge the text, or they use their browser settings to zoom in on the entire page. When the presentation is designed for flexibility, the information design is clear in any display.

- **Information structure is communicated in more than one way.** People usually think of information design in visual terms, such as how elements are arranged in an information space: they use visual cues, such as alignment and white space, to guide the eye through information and interactive elements. But you cannot rely on just one sense—in this example, vision—to communicate meaning. Users may not have access to information conveyed visually, or they may have changed the display to meet their own needs, thereby changing the information design.

- **The visual design makes content easier to read.** Medical and rehabilitation research on how people learn to read suggests that some problems with literacy have their roots in visual ability and how the brain processes text. For example, unsteady eye movements can make it hard to keep track of the line of words being read, or poor binocular vision can make letters appear to move around. Good contrast and line spacing, white space around content, and even the shorter sentences recommended in plain language guidelines help people read more easily (see Chapter 8, "Plain Language").

Carol

Why can't the text be just a little bit larger?

I've always loved reading, but my eyesight has been going for years. Now, it's getting worse with this macular degeneration in one eye. A friend gave me a magnifier that she used for needlework. It sits over my book, so my hands are free. That helped for a long time. But even though I'm not very good at using the computer, I still like to try, especially to see the photos my grandkids send me. I love keeping up with them that way.

Some sites have text that's just so small. I don't know what I can do. I've learned how to set up my browser so that the text is bigger. It makes the links bigger, too, so I can click on them more easily. I wish all the sites would do this. Some just don't seem to work. The text stays the same size, and I can't read it at all.

How to Design for Clean Presentation

A clean design with the goal of accessibility starts by applying best practices for information and graphic design, which benefit all users. Since software is an important "user," you need to apply those best practices both on the surface and in the code, so information structure can be conveyed to nonvisual users. And you need to design for flexibility, so the information design remains easy to understand and use, even in different display formats.

Design simply

To design simply is to design with restraint. Unfortunately, there are many competing factors that must be considered in a design, and business concerns can too easily win over user needs. Clients may request "flashy" designs that "pop" as they look for ways to stand out from competitors. But simplicity can be a great differentiator, where important elements stand out and the site stays true to purpose (see Chapter 3, "Clear Purpose," *Design for clarity and simplicity*).

In addition, simple designs are easier to make responsive to different devices and display formats.

In general:

- **Simple designs are stable and coherent.** Each element in the design is necessary to the overall information and functionality. Simplicity provides a sense of unity to the elements of the design.
- **Consistent designs are easier to use because, once learned, the interaction model can be applied throughout the product.** For example, websites that have the same functional element, like the search field, in different locations through the site require that the user relearn the interface on each page.
- **Design conventions can help with usability because we all know how they work.** For example, when a group of controls on the screen are surrounded by a visual box, we know they are related to one another—and this relationship can be encoded in the document.
- **Design patterns are also helpful.** No need to reinvent the wheel for the sake of creativity—at least, not in the site or app framework. Using conventions and patterns makes the design more consistent.

Minimize distracting clutter

Distractions and clutter make it difficult to concentrate on the task at hand. With a cluttered design, the user begins working with a page by first developing a strategy for identifying relevant items and tuning out distractions. For people with disabilities that affect concentration and comprehension, this need may be keener, and developing a strategy may require more effort.

Unfortunately, business requirements and client expectations often lead to cluttered designs. When adding a new feature to a design that is already cluttered, one way to draw attention is to add motion of some sort. And with the next new feature, more motion, and so on.

You only have one chance to make a good first impression. On a website or web application, first impressions are a deciding factor in whether people stay or go. The longer people stay, the more likely they are having an enjoyable experience.

Several eye-tracking research studies have shown that users scan the page and make their decision about where to focus in about 2.6 seconds. In one study, users were shown screenshots of websites for law schools. They spent an average of 20 seconds on each one. The areas of the page that drew their interest included:

- The institution's logo (6.48 seconds)
- The main navigation menu (6.44 seconds)
- The search box (6 seconds)
- Social networking links to sites such as Facebook and Twitter (5.95 seconds)
- The site's main image (5.94 seconds)
- The site's written content (5.59 seconds)
- The bottom of a website (5.25 seconds)

Participants were then asked to rate sites based on their design. The researchers found that the longer they stayed on the page "the more favorable their impressions were. First impressions are important for keeping people on pages."

"Eye-tracking Studies: First Impressions Form Quickly on the Web," Missouri University of Science and Technology. http://news.mst.edu/2012/02/ eye-tracking_studies_show_firs/

Ultimately, meeting business needs means satisfying user needs by providing the most direct path to relevant content and functionality. You don't want a user's first impression of your site to be, "Whoa! How do I cope with this design?" So try to minimize clutter, avoid elements that move or auto-play, and provide clear access to the features that users want.

See Chapter 5, "Easy Interaction," *Let users control the operation of the interface* and Chapter 9, *Use dynamic elements carefully* for more on minimizing clutter.

Design for customization of the display

One person's "clean" is another's "clutter"—it's impossible to create a design that will work perfectly for all users. Fortunately, the web is a flexible medium, unlike paper or physical products. It's also a user-controlled medium that responds first and foremost to user settings. While web designers provide a starting point, or default design, along

The wild clutter of features and ads, especially on content pages, has produced a market for web page de-cluttering tools. Readability is a service that, according to Fast Company's John Pavlus, "transforms any article, blog post, or long feature from a Flash-addled, ad-encrusted headache into a calm, humane ... readable experience."[1] Readability works on the understanding that reading requires a level of focus that cannot be achieved with extraneous elements competing for attention. To remove distractions, Readability software pulls out the main content of a page and displays it in a clean, customizable format (see Figure 7.1).

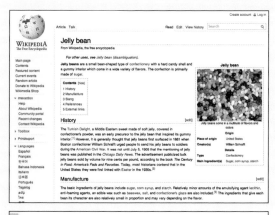

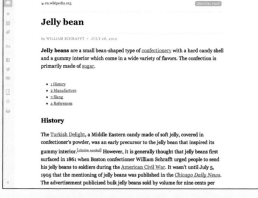

FIGURE 7.1
Readability removes everything on the page except the main content so that readers are not distracted. (www.readability.com)

---

1 http://www.fastcodesign.com/1663138/with-clever-ui-readability-hopes-to-please-readers-into-paying-more

For users, flexible layouts work best because they can adjust designs to fit certain criteria; for example, by enlarging the default text size in browser preferences. Fixed designs make it harder for users to adapt their view.

For designers who want to be able to control the visual presentation precisely, flexible designs are harder to embrace. One approach to designing for different devices has been to create fixed designs that display well in different contexts. However, it's costly to have several versions to maintain.

Enter Responsive Web Design! RWD allows for one codebase containing the content of the page, with instructions for multiple layouts for different size screens. This approach has gained traction with designers and developers, and supports flexibility for accessibility, too. Flexible at its core, it allows for some control over how pages look and behave in different contexts. (See the profile in this chapter, *Responsive Design with Ethan Marcotte*, for details from the RWD inventor himself.)

RWD appeals to designers because it allows them to be both flexible and design to a grid. Layout grids bring balance and consistency to a design. Grid dimensions are usually based on fixed values derived from the dimensions of the output. Whether business card, poster, or billboard, a symmetrical layout grid based on the width/height ratio of the final printed size is a dependable way to position elements in a design.

But what about layout grids in a flexible environment like the web, where output dimensions are unknown? How can users enjoy the benefits of balance and consistency and still customize the display?

In his 2009 A List Apart article, Ethan Marcotte found a way to create a grid based on relative measures (ems) that would adjust while keeping the relative proportions of the design. Using the formula target ÷ context = result, he showed how to arrive at the correct em value to use to size different elements of the design.

Say you are aiming for a heading sized at 24 pixels (target). You know the standard default text size in most browsers is 16 pixels (context). Plug those numbers into the formula, and you get 24 ÷ 16 = 1.5, or the CSS declaration font-size: 1.5em. You can use the same formula to get relative values to define the size of page elements.

Flexible grids create balanced and coherent layouts that adapt when users customize their display or use different devices. Figure 7.2 shows an example of a page in four different views.

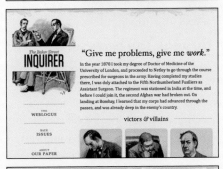

FIGURE 7.2
Elements in Ethan's
fluid grid example page
(headings, columns,
margins) maintain their
relative proportions
when text is enlarged
using the Zoom feature
in Firefox. (www.
alistapart.com/d/
responsive-web-design/
ex/ex-site-flexible.html)

with page content, users determine how the content displays. But that works only when designs are coded with flexibility in mind.

Flexible designs start by separating content from presentation (see Chapter 4, "Solid Structure," *Use semantic markup for content*). This separation allows the content to adapt to different displays because the design instructions are in a stylesheet rather than embedded in the content. This separation allows browsers to use different instructions for different contexts and user needs.

Design for flexibility requires more than just stylesheets. There are many aspects of a design that are affected by different contexts. For example, when a user changes the width of the browser window, the page is redisplayed to fit. Using relative measures, like ems or percentages, results in a page that adapts better when users enlarge type size or view a page on large and small screens. No one wins when text overlaps or the whole side of the page is cut off and the page is unreadable.

A customizable design is the most effective approach for people with vision disabilities, as their needs are diverse and cannot be addressed with any one design. Instead, try to create a design with flexibility in mind that retains its integrity, functionality, and content while allowing users to make necessary changes to its visual display.

Support customization through the browser

Some websites include customization features to allow users to adjust the display directly on the website—for example, by enlarging the text, changing color settings, and adjusting page width and number of columns. To some extent, these are helpful, although it's a bit like providing reading glasses along with a book. People visit many websites and will likely arrive at yours with their glasses in place—that is, running necessary software and with their browser and operating system settings configured to meet their needs and preferences.

Recently, leading sites like the BBC (**www.bbc.co.uk/accessibility**) have taken a different approach. First, they build their sites to standards, so they work with all the built-in features of the browsers. Then, instead of building custom controls for flexibility, their accessibility Help pages teach users how to use those features to adjust the display for all sites.

Most importantly, be sure that any changes to the presentation, such as text size or zoom, fonts and text colors, or set language options, work across all the pages on your site. Imagine having to reset the text size on every page.

Customizable Designs for Low-Vision Users

In 2003, Mary Frances Theofanos and Ginny Redish conducted a research study with a group of users whose vision was impaired enough to require screen magnification software. Vision disabilities varied among the participants, from congenital to those types that come with aging. An important outcome from the study was the following insight: "The needs of low-vision users are too diverse for simple solutions to web accessibility and usability."

They found that flexibility is key, creating designs that respond to customizations and configurations that are tuned to individual needs. And while they stressed that simple solutions were not possible, their design guidelines for low-vision users provided a good starting point:

- Never rely on color alone to convey functional meaning—that includes not relying on background color alone to define different sections of a web page.
- Outline tabs with a black border so that they look like tabs even when their special colors are taken away.
- Do not use graphic images for textual elements like links.
- Use relative sizes for text, not absolute sizes.
- Check stylesheets and fonts on actual pages to be sure that all the text enlarges properly.
- Use sans serif type for websites.

From "Helping Low-vision and Other Users with Web Sites That Meet Their Needs: Is One Site for All Feasible?" by Mary Theofanos and Janice (Ginny) Redish, in *Technical Communication* 52 (1), 2005. http://archive.stc.org/Pubs/tech-comm.asp Used with permission.

People with some vision disabilities need specific color combinations or amounts of contrast between the text and background. For these users, the simple contrast requirements in the WCAG 2.0 are not enough to make the page accessible. Instead, they use high-contrast modes, such as an inverted color scheme; for example, perhaps a black background with yellow text. Many browser settings for high contrast also remove background colors and images, so that there is a uniform color behind the text. This means that any content or interface elements provided by the background disappears.

If I can adjust my screen, I can read comfortably.

I use a smaller window than I used to, because my vision kind of fades out at the edges. When I can, I make the whole page larger, so I can see the details in images better, too. Once I find a site that I can set up to read well, I stick with it—the BBC for international news, a cricket site. What I really want is for the web to look the way I need it to, not just a few favorite sites.

Vishnu

Design content for easy comprehension

It's difficult to separate "content" into "words" and "presentation" because they are both critical for making content easy to scan and understand. In Chapter 8, you'll learn how words, sentences, and paragraphs can be written for accessibility. But you also need to think about how the information is presented.

A large, undifferentiated block of text is like a wall of words—uninviting, difficult to read and understand, and potentially a barrier. Information that is broken up into logical sections is more inviting and accessible, and much easier to scan.

Start by breaking the content into meaningful chunks:

- **Break up blocks of text** into short paragraphs with headings, following good practice for plain language.
- **Use bullets and tables** appropriately to make lists easy to identify and scan.
- **Group similar items** with design elements that separate them from other items on the page.

Then use semantic markup to encode the information hierarchy of the page:

- **Use heading tags** (<h1> to <h6>) in the correct order.
- **Use list and table markup,** for lists and tables only.
- **Use semantic tags** (such as <fieldset> and <nav> and ARIA roles like "navigation" and "banner") to group information by function.

See Chapter 4, *Use semantic markup for content* and Chapter 6, "Helpful Wayfinding," *Provide clear landmarks within the page* for more information on how to code for semantic meaning that allows assistive technology to work effectively.

The Center for Plain Language considers the layout to be as important as the words in helping readers understand a document or web page. Their checklist for evaluating plain language includes this set of guidelines for the visual design:

The design reinforces meaning and makes it easier for the audience to see, process, and use the information. Consider if the design:

- Organizes the information in a sequence that's logical for the audience.
- Uses layout to make information easy to find, understand, and use.
- Uses principles of good design—including appropriate typography, font size, line spacing, color, white space, and so on.
- Uses visuals to make concepts, information, and links easier to see and understand.
- For online information, minimizes the number of levels.
- For online information, layers information appropriately, avoiding too much on one page.

http://centerforplainlanguage.org/about-plain-language/checklist/

Use color contrast to separate foreground from background

Without contrast, the whole world would just be gray. The design needs to meet color contrast requirements for people with vision or color perception deficiencies. Color combinations that are easily distinguishable to someone with normal vision may not work at all for people with one of the many types of visual disabilities. Contrast perception can also be reduced due to environmental factors, such as display settings and light conditions.

To distinguish the foreground elements, there must be sufficient color contrast between the foreground and background. Too little contrast between the text and background reduces legibility and causes fatigue for readers.

To provide enough contrast, you have to maximize color differences. Black and white have the greatest contrast, since white has 100% lightness and black has 0% lightness. Here are a few guidelines for creating good contrast:

- **Choose complementary colors,** or colors from opposing sides of the color circle

- **Choose colors with different degrees of lightness,** such as a light color from the top half of the circle with a dark color from the bottom half of the circle

- **Make the font large enough.** Use more contrast for text in a smaller font. If you are using a light color on a dark background, the text must be larger or bolder, especially for reading on a computer screen.

- **Avoid using only a pastel background** to separate blocks of information. Pale backgrounds may not be visible to people with color perception disabilities. Combine background colors with borders, rules, extra white space, or other visual elements.

A quick way to check color contrast is by looking at the presentation in grayscale (see Figure 7.3). The WCAG 2.0 guidelines include acceptable values for color contrast for both large and small text, since small text requires more contrast for legibility. Fortunately, testing for sufficient color contrast is easy. There are tools, like the Color Contrast Analyzer, which allow you to verify color combinations. When the default colors in the design have enough contrast, fewer people need to rely on customizing their browser settings, making the design more universal.

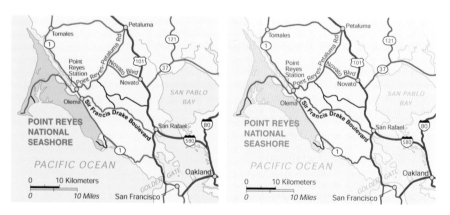

FIGURE 7.3

Good contrast is not just for accessibility. It's a great way to make sure that your page or infographics will print well on a grayscale printer. Notice that even though this image has both red and green, the highly saturated red is still visible against the lighter green in the grayscale image. (Image from NISTIR-7537: "Guidelines for Using Color in Voting Systems")

The formatting of tables can make a big difference in how readable the information is. In a study comparing different ways of presenting tabular data, Tom Tullis and Stan Fleischman found that a larger font, loose spacing, and alternate color rows helped participants find specific information more accurately and efficiently than using lines around the cells (see Figure 7.4).

A few years later, Jessica Enders took a look at the common practice of "zebra striping" or displaying alternate rows in a table with different background colors. When she ran an experiment, she did not find strongly improved accuracy or speed. However, participants preferred tables with alternating background colors.

Name	Thread pitch (mm)	Minor diameter tolerance	Nominal diameter (mm)	Head shape	Price for 50 screws	Available at factory outlet?	Number in stock	Flat or Phillips head?
M4	0.7	4g	4	Pan	$10.08	Yes	276	Flat
M5	0.8	4g	5	Round	$13.89	Yes	183	Both
M6	1	5g	6	Button	$10.42	Yes	1043	Flat
M8	1.25	5g	8	Pan	$11.98	No	298	Phillips
M10	1.5	6g	10	Round	$16.74	Yes	488	Phillips
M12	1.75	7g	12	Pan	$18.26	No	998	Flat
M14	2	7g	14	Round	$21.19	No	235	Phillips
M16	2	8g	16	Button	$23.57	Yes	292	Both
M18	2.1	8g	18	Button	$25.87	No	664	Both
M20	2.4	8g	20	Pan	$29.09	Yes	486	Both
M24	2.55	9g	24	Round	$33.01	Yes	982	Phillips
M28	2.7	10g	28	Button	$35.66	No	1067	Phillips
M36	3.2	12g	36	Pan	$41.32	No	434	Both
M50	4.5	15g	50	Pan	$44.72	No	740	Flat

FIGURE 7.4

This table uses both zebra striping and the loose spacing that Tullis and Fleischman recommend.

"Tabular Data: Finding the Best Format" by Tom Tullis and Stan Fleischman, *Intercom*, June 2004. www.tullisfamily.org/TomTullis/TabularData.pdf

"Zebra Striping: Does It Really Help?" by Jessica Enders, A List Apart, May 6, 2008. http://alistapart.com/article/zebrastripingdoesithelp

"Zebra Striping: More Data for the Case" by Jessica Enders, A List Apart, September 9, 2008. http://alistapart.com/article/zebrastripingmoredataforthecase

Contrast can be tricky to check when the background is a texture or image because each letter may be used against several different background colors. It is also more difficult for people to read text against a varied background. Use a solid background behind text.

Use visual and semantic space

The neutral space between elements brings clarity to a design, making it easy to see the sequence and relatedness of design elements. Neutral, blank space is created visually with the style settings for margins, line height, indents, and blank lines. Using markup creates "space" semantically by identifying each element separately.

For example, in a navigation menu, you use white space to visually separate each menu item and to separate the menu from other page elements. In the code, you perform the same delimiting function, enclosing each menu item in an `<li>` tag and separating the menu from other content with `<ul>` and `<nav>` tags.

White space helps everyone make sense of a design. Using semantic markup makes the function of white space programmatically determinable. (For more on sectioning markup see the table in Chapter 4, *Sectioning markup to group and label*).

Provide enough space between lines of text

Line spacing, or *leading*, is another facet of white space that impacts accessibility (see Figure 7.5). Sometimes called *line-height,* leading is the distance from the baseline of one line of text to the next. The amount of

Narrow
line-height: 120%

> **Jelly bean**
> Jelly beans are a small bean-shaped type of confectionery with a hard candy shell and a gummy interior which come in a wide variety of flavors. The confection is primarily made of sugar.
>
> **History**
> The Turkish Delight, a Middle Eastern candy made of soft jelly, covered in confectioner's powder, was an early precursor to the jelly bean that inspired its gummy interior. However, it is generally thought that jelly beans first surfaced in 1861 when Boston confectioner William Schrafft urged people to send his jelly beans to soldiers during the American Civil War. It wasn't until July 5, 1905 that the mentioning of jelly beans was published in the Chicago Daily News. The advertisement publicized bulk jelly beans sold by volume for nine cents per pound, according to the book, "The Century in Food: America's Fads and Favorites." Today, most historians contend that in the United States, they were first linked with Easter in the 1930s.
>
> **Manufacture**
> The basic ingredients of jelly beans include sugars, corn syrup, and starch. Relatively minor amounts of the emulsifying agent lecithin, anti-foaming agents,

Medium
line-height: 150%

> **Jelly bean**
> Jelly beans are a small bean-shaped type of confectionery with a hard candy shell and a gummy interior which come in a wide variety of flavors. The confection is primarily made of sugar.
>
> **History**
> The Turkish Delight, a Middle Eastern candy made of soft jelly, covered in confectioner's powder, was an early precursor to the jelly bean that inspired its gummy interior. However, it is generally thought that jelly beans first surfaced in 1861 when Boston confectioner William Schrafft urged people to send his jelly beans to soldiers during the American Civil War. It wasn't until July 5, 1905 that the mentioning of jelly beans was published in the Chicago Daily News. The advertisement publicized bulk jelly beans sold by volume for nine cents per pound, according to the book, "The Century in Food: America's Fads and Favorites." Today, most historians contend that in the United States, they were first linked with Easter in the 1930s.

Wide
line-height: 180%

> **Jelly bean**
> Jelly beans are a small bean-shaped type of confectionery with a hard candy shell and a gummy interior which come in a wide variety of flavors. The confection is primarily made of sugar.
>
> **History**
> The Turkish Delight, a Middle Eastern candy made of soft jelly, covered in confectioner's powder, was an early precursor to the jelly bean that inspired its gummy interior. However, it is generally thought that jelly beans first surfaced in 1861 when Boston confectioner William Schrafft urged people to send his jelly beans to soldiers during the American Civil War. It wasn't until July 5, 1905 that the mentioning of jelly beans was published in the Chicago Daily News. The advertisement publicized bulk jelly beans sold by volume for nine cents per pound, according to the book, "The Century in Food: America's Fads and

FIGURE 7.5

Line spacing is like the three bears: it's important that it's not too narrow or too wide—both make text harder to read.

white space between lines of text influences how effectively you track from the end of one line to the beginning of the next. Too little space can cause the text to overlap. Too much space can make it hard to move your eye to the next line. It's best to express line height as a percentage of font size, so that leading will adjust based on the user's preferred text size.

Use clean typography

A clean typographic style gives stability and clarity to a design, and it also enhances readability. Readability is an important consideration, particularly for users who have difficulty reading or who use software that makes reading more difficult.

- **Use a clear, easy-to-read typeface.** Sans-serif fonts with distinct letter shapes help people with dyslexia and other vision disabilities read more easily. Fonts like Arial, Century Gothic, Verdana, and Trebuchet (and fonts with a similar typeface design) work well. Fonts that have a large x-height (the height of a lowercase "x") fare best on screen.

- **Text alignment creates stability in a design and defines relationships among elements.** Left-aligned text is more readable because the consistent left margin creates a stable anchor for tracking through lines of text.

- **Stick with one or two fonts in the design.** Avoid adjustments to type, such as condensed or tightened letter spacing, as they can make the text run together.

- **Typographic emphasis draws attention to elements—bold, uppercase, italics, underlining, and color.** For clear presentation, emphasis must be conveyed in the code of the page so it is available to software. Also, emphasis should be used sparingly. Too many elements competing for attention make it hard to focus. Use underlining only for links.

Note that uppercase letters are effective at getting attention—often too effective, as they seem to be shouting. Also, uppercase words are not particularly legible because we are used to reading text in a mix of uppercase and lowercase letters. We read the shapes of words, as well as the letters, and uppercase words are shapeless. It's best to avoid setting text in all uppercase. Figure 7.6 shows a dramatic metaphor for the value of mixed case type we saw in a presentation by Drew Davies from Design for Democracy.

FIGURE 7.6
When everything is the same height, it's hard to tell what's going on in the landscape, but with a variation in shape, color, and height, features are easy to distinguish.

Who Is Responsible for Clean Presentation?

Information and graphic designers take the lead in the quest for clean presentation. Collaboration with others, however, is essential. The content team should also be involved in creating the stylesheet, to ensure that the styles support clear communication and provide enough variation to meet the content needs on the site.

The development team should code presentation elements in an accessible manner, so the site presents well across browsers, devices, and assistive technology.

WCAG 2.0 and Clean Presentation

The guidelines for Clean Presentation map to the following WCAG 2.0 requirements.

A site with clean presentation is **Perceivable**, allowing users to customize the presentation to their own needs.

A site with clean presentation meets the guidelines:

- **1.3 Adaptable:** Create content that can be presented in different ways (for example simpler layout) without losing information or structure (Guideline).
- **1.4 Distinguishable:** Make it easier for users to see and hear content including separating foreground from background (Guideline).

Fonts matter for reading disabilities like dyslexia. Several designers around the world have created fonts aimed at improving reading and writing for people with dyslexia. In fonts like Read Regular, shown in Figure 7.7, the letters are all designed with shapes that make them easier to distinguish. They use:

- Clear, simple character shapes without unnecessary details or embellishments.

- Distinctive shapes, especially for characters that are similar, such as "b" and "d" and "p" and "q."

- Long ascenders and descenders to emphasize the difference in the letters.

- Good spacing between the letters, so that shapes like "r," "n," and "m" don't run together.

- Wider openings in letters to make them easier to recognize.

```
abcdefghijklmnopqrstuvwxyz
ABCDEFGHIJKLMNOPQRSTUVWXYZ
0123456789
,.!'?'(...)"[&]"{*%@}
```

Read Regular © Natascha Frensch 2001-2012

FIGURE 7.7
Sample of the Read Regular typeface, created by Natascha Frensch, a graphic designer at the Royal College of Art in the UK. (www.readregular.com/english/regular.html)

The requirements for clean presentation are:

- **1.3.1 Info and Relationships:** Information, structure, and relationships conveyed through presentation can be programmatically determined, or are available in text (Level A).

- **1.4.3 and 1.4.6 Contrast:** The visual presentation of text and images of text has a contrast ratio of at least 4.5:1 or 3:1 for large text (Level AA) *or* 7:1 or 4.5:1 for large text (Level AAA) except for logos and decorative images.

- **1.4.4 Resize text:** Except for captions and images of text, text can be resized without assistive technology up to 200 percent without loss of content or functionality (Level AA).

- **1.4.5 and 1.4.9 Images of Text:** Text is used to convey information rather than images of text (Level AAA) or with exceptions for cases where the presentation is essential to the meaning (Level AA).
- **1.4.8 Visual Presentation:** For the visual presentation of blocks of text, users can adjust the contrast, text size (Level AAA).
  - Text can be resized without assistive technology up to 200 percent in a way that does not require the user to scroll horizontally to read a line of text on a full-screen window.
  - Line spacing (leading) is at least space-and-a-half within paragraphs, and paragraph spacing is at least 1.5 times larger than the line spacing.
  - Width is no more than 80 characters or glyphs (40 if CJK).
  - Text is not justified (aligned to both the left and the right margins).
- **2.4.6 Headings and Labels:** Headings and labels describe topic or purpose (Level AA).
- **2.4.10 Section Headings:** Section headings are used to organize the content (Level AAA).
- **3.3.2 Labels or Instructions:** Labels or instructions are provided when content requires user input (Level A).

The full text of the WCAG 2.0 requirements can be found in Appendix B.

Summary

A clean presentation enhances the usability of the site for everyone by designing the visual layout and typography for easy perception. However, to ensure that the presentation is accessible for the wide variety of visual disabilities, the site must also be designed to allow users to customize the look, either through the browser or through controls built into the site.

A site with well-designed stylesheets not only supports user requirements, but also allows the presentation to adjust in response to the device and screen size. This sort of flexibility is important to both accessibility and responsive design.

Elements of the presentation that are especially important for accessibility are the contrast between the text and background, the fonts used, the text size, line spacing, and the use of white space to make areas of the screen easy to differentiate.

Ethan Marcotte is a designer who codes and a coder who designs. While many web professionals have this combined skill set, Ethan brings a high level of mastery to both disciplines. And like all great masters, Ethan is also a teacher. Ethan literally wrote the book on a flexible design approach called "responsive design." We wanted to learn from Ethan how a flexible approach supports accessibility.

Ethan started his career in the late 1990s, and has worked in design studios for most of his career, including several years as Interactive Design Director for the award-winning design studio, Happy Cog. Currently, he runs his own web practice, and has worked for a variety of clients including Stanford University, Sundance Film Festival, and New York Magazine. *He worked on a large-scale and ground-breaking design of the* Boston Globe, *with Filament Group, in which he employed the "flexibility in use" principle in a design approach he invented.*

Balancing control and flexibility through responsive design.

"Flexibility is near and dear to my heart." Ethan's early career was spent creating flat graphics in Photoshop or Illustrator, and then implementing the design in code. "I started off building sites that were 620 pixels wide, then 760, then 960. Every couple of years, there was a universal consensus established: 'Okay, now it's safe to upgrade.' But natively the web doesn't understand width or height or anything like that." This disconnect got him thinking about a more flexible approach.

The essay by John Allsopp, "A Dao of Web Design," helped Ethan see that by bringing preconceptions to the web based on a completely different medium—print—designers were getting in the way of the flexibility inherent in the web. And that flexibility was key to accessibility. Ethan began to explore ways to achieve "controlled flexibility" in web design, a place somewhere between absolute flexibility and absolute control.

> *What is so fundamentally powerful about the web is that promise of access. We have the technology and approach in place to design sites that are as viewable on a feature phone as they are on a 27-inch monitor with the latest Chrome browser. Flexibility doesn't require a sacrifice in the quality of the experience on one end or the other. It's all about delivering content to people.*

Ethan says that content delivery is the primary goal of a responsive design approach: making sure that content is universally accessible, regardless of how it is accessed. It starts with structured HTML for content, and then uses CSS and JavaScript to progressively enhance the experience. HTML5 media queries provide the opportunity to "tune the display," adapting elements such as color and size, depending on the needs of the user.

profile continues on next page

"Responsive design is really just a new name for a lot of old thinking about capitalizing on the flexibility inherent in the web." It's an approach that looks at flexibility "not as something we need to work around or constrain, but rather as an opportunity to enhance the design."

In essence, responsive design is about "bringing the design to meet the users."

Redesigning the *Boston Globe* website.

Ethan and his colleagues at Filament Group implemented responsive design on the *Boston Globe* website. "It was a seriously fun project. There were a lot of interesting problems to solve. And the *Globe* was really committed to the idea of making their content as universally accessible as possible."

> *We didn't want to think about accessibility at the end of the project, as is usually the case. We tried to think broadly throughout the process, and work proactively rather than reactively.*

Rather than working from a list of browsers and devices, they focused on characteristics, such as the size of the screen, the input model, and the availability of technologies such as CSS and JavaScript. For example, rather than testing how a carousel would work on a specific device, they asked how it would be accessible to someone who didn't have JavaScript. For each type of display or interaction, they established a baseline for accessible content, and used progressive enhancement techniques to enhance the experience for more capable systems.

The new bostonglobe.com, launched in September of 2011, has been cited as a "major step in the evolution of website design," (Beaconfire) providing an "elegant, readable website no matter what screen size you're using." (Webmonkey) It even displays cleanly on an Apple Newton. "It's structured HTML—there are headings, paragraphs, lists. You can still browse the site. That's a testament to the portability of the technologies we work with."

Ahead: More opportunities for responsiveness.

Looking ahead, Ethan sees more opportunities to build responsiveness into websites and web applications, including new CSS3 modules like flex box and grid layout, which will allow greater control over the display order of elements. But in order to move forward with a responsive approach, he believes that we need to revise our expectations about control. For so long, design efforts have been about "slotting paragraphs into specific positions on pages." For universally accessible content, Ethan urges that designers work with the native flexibility of the web, rather than trying to constrain it. "If your web app is a call to one JavaScript function that spits out HTML to the page, think about what that experience is going to be like for less capable browsers and readers. If you think flexibly from the outset, it makes a lot of things much easier."

CHAPTER 8

Plain Language: Creates a Conversation

Medicare Summary Notice

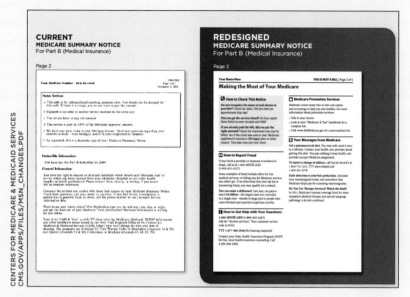

The redesigned Medicare Summary Notice letter is not only rewritten in plain language, but also formatted with headings and good use of clean design principles. You can see the whole letter, showing before and after, online. (www.cms.gov/apps/files/msn_changes.pdf)

We've all seen information that is incomprehensible. Sometimes it's what plain language advocates call *gobbledegook*—information written in complex sentences, full of jargon, and usually presented in a wall of words.

The Medicare Summary Notice from the U.S. government is a good example of an unusable government form letter that has been improved through plain language. This letter is sent to anyone in the U.S. who receives medical benefits covered by Medicare— mostly older adults and people with disabilities. A press release describing the new design focused on the impact for citizens: "The new Medicare Summary Notice empowers Medicare's seniors and people with disabilities. The statement is easier to understand and navigate, and makes clear what information to check." (www.cms.gov/apps/files/msn_changes.pdf)

Information is critical for all of us, whether reading content or using an application. If you can't read and understand the information, then it might as well not be there. And, if it's confusing, the content can be a barrier, leading to mistakes.

In thinking about language in a universal design context, it's important to remember that plain language is not just a list of rules for grammar. Plain language also includes information design—how the information is presented as well as how it is written. Be sure to consider the strategies for presenting text in Chapter 7, "Clean Presentation," when designing or creating web content.

How Plain Language Supports Accessibility

Plain language is important to accessibility because cognitive disabilities and low reading literacy are relatively common, and because people read with different levels of literacy. Literacy includes a wide range of abilities, from understanding the words themselves to being able to assemble those words into meaningful information.

An International Definition of Plain Language

The definition from the U.S. Center for Plain Language (and adopted by other organizations around the world) focuses on the audience:

When you write in plain language, you create information that works well for the people who use it, whether online or in print.

Our measure of plain language is behavioral: Can the people who are the audience for the material quickly and easily:

- Find what they need?
- Understand what they find?
- Act appropriately on that understanding?

This means that the definition of "plain" depends on the audience. What is plain language for one audience may not be plain language for another audience.

Center for Plain Language: centerforplainlanguage.org/about-plain-language/

With plain language, **people can read, understand, and use the information.**

- **Information is easy to understand, even in poor conditions.** As much as we would like to think that everyone reads every word we write ... they don't. People are in a hurry, get distracted, or miss a critical word in a paragraph. They may be scanning a page quickly, multi-tasking, or be interrupted.

  People also read in places that make reading more difficult. We are often in motion when we read direction and wayfinding signs, even if only at walking speeds. We read websites in places with poor lighting, in bright sunlight, and on mobile devices with tiny screens (and tiny text). All of these situations create contextual, temporary impairment of our ability to read easily. Writing in plain language means that content is structured to support everyone, even careless, rushed readers.

- **The site supports a wider audience.** It's easy to focus on differences between audiences, but when it comes to the need for plain language, people—even from very different audiences—may be more alike than we think. For example, in a project for the Open University, Whitney and Caroline Jarrett were asked whether the university needed separate sites for different kinds of students. At first glance, teens leaving secondary school, older adults looking for new educational challenges, and people (often with weaker English language skills) looking for a way up the economic ladder didn't seem very similar. A review of the research confirmed this, suggesting a very different picture of each group.

  When they dug into suggested guidelines for how to write and design for each audience, they found that the different audiences had similar guidelines, even though they started from different characteristics (see Table 8.1).

  While the guidelines are not exactly the same, the same issues come up for each audience, and suggest similar ways of making information clear and usable for different people. For example, all of them suggested sticking to words the audience knows, writing with short, clear sentences, and using illustrations meaningfully. (The references to these guidelines are in Appendix C, "More Reading.")

- **The site supports a global audience and people reading in translation.** The web is global. Many people read websites in a second (or third) language. Guidelines for plain language support non-native readers, and also make information easier to translate.

TABLE 8.1 DIFFERENT AUDIENCES: SIMILAR GUIDELINES

Audience	Aptitude and Ability	Guidelines
Teens	Impatient browsers with short attention spans, too distracted to read small print carefully.	Write simply, using words that are common to your readers' vocabulary. Be concise and get to the point. Use images that add meaning and illustrate concepts visually.
Older Adults	Often slower, more careful, and hesitant browsers, "cautious clickers" who read every word on the screen.	Use words that most older adults know. Write with short, simple, and straightforward sentences. Use captions or meaningful alternative text for images.
Low Literacy	Slower readers who focus on the central content of the page, skipping chunks of content when they don't understand them.	Use appropriate vocabulary. Write text with a simple sentence structure. Keep pages, paragraphs, sentences short. Use information graphics and animations to show processes and relationships.

Vishnu

Translating in my head is easier with simpler sentences.

In my field—we're working on medical imaging for diagnostic testing—the professional papers are in English. No matter what language we speak in our daily lives, everyone in my company reads two other languages: software mathematics and English. It's the international language. The concepts are complicated, so I really appreciate it when I find a paper where they are presented in clear language. It's not just reading the paper itself—searching and navigating in English can be harder than reading the technical papers, where at least I know the jargon.

How to Design for Plain Language

Designing content is not so different than designing any other aspect of a website. Even if project teams don't usually talk about "designing content," perhaps they should.

Principles from previous chapters apply to plain language:

- **Clear purpose:** Know what you are trying to say.
- **Solid structure:** Use semantic markup for content elements.
- **Clean presentation:** Make content readable in both words and design,

Write for your audience

Like everything else about usability and accessibility, plain language starts from people, and making information appropriate for the audience. On today's web, we design (and write) for diverse, sometimes large audiences. Writing in plain language does not mean oversimplifying or dumbing down the content. But even technical audiences appreciate clear communication that gets to the point, with content that is easy to understand instead of convoluted sentences and overblown language.

Finding a universal language may be difficult when there is a wide audience, but the effort pays off in making it easier for all visitors to understand the information on the site. After all, assistive technology can't change the words as easily as a stylesheet can change the font, size, or color of the text … yet.

Follow plain language guidelines for writing content

Writing content in plain language focuses on the readers. You want them to *find*, *understand*, and *use* the information, so you make sure they can read quickly and accurately.

You might also think that writing for the web is different than other writing, but research suggests that guidelines for print and web are very similar. The differences are based on the genre or the type of information being presented. The important consideration for deciding which guidelines to follow is the type of information, especially for information that appears both in print and online.

Types of Literacy

Literacy is not just a question of being able to read, but also whether the reader can understand and act on the information. The U.S. National Assessment of Adult Literacy identifies three types of literacy as they measure how well adults can use printed and written communication in their daily lives.

- **Prose literacy:** Reading and using information in prose form, such as brochures, news stories, or instructional materials.

- **Document literacy:** Reading and using noncontinuous texts in formats such as job applications, payroll forms, transportation schedules, or drug and food labels.

- **Quantitative literacy:** Identifying, understanding, and performing computations such as balancing a checkbook, calculating a tip, or completing an order form.

Looking across all three types of literacy, they identified four levels of literacy:

- **Below basic:** The most simple and concrete literacy skills, such as searching a short, simple text to find out what a patient is allowed to drink before a medical test.

- **Basic:** Skills necessary to perform simple and everyday literacy activities, such as comparing ticket prices for two events or reading a pamphlet for jurors.

- **Intermediate:** Ability to perform moderately challenging literacy activities including using quantitative information to solve problems, like calculating the total cost of ordering specific office supplies from a catalog.

- **Proficient:** Skills necessary to perform more complex and challenging literacy activities, such as interpreting a table about blood pressure, age, and physical activity.

The latest report shows that 14% of adults in the U.S. have below basic levels of prose literacy. For more statistics and how the data was collected, you can read the 2003 National Assessment of Adult Literacy, http://nces.ed.gov/naal/

Organize the information from the reader's perspective. Put the sections of the site, page, section or sentence in a logical order for your readers. Order is especially important for instructions, but this guideline applies to any information. Think about what information your readers need first.

Put the "if" before the "then." Make sure that the context is clear right at the beginning of the sentence or paragraph. Putting information in the right order is a kind of wayfinding at the sentence level, helping users figure out whether they need to read the rest of the conversation. Putting information in a logical order makes it more accessible to people who don't read well, who read slowly, or who are listening to content in audio.

- Use introductory phrases or sentences to announce the topic before you dive into the details.

- If you are listing options, put the condition first, then what happens in this situation. ("If you are sending a gift, write the message for the gift card here.")

- If the options are for people in different roles, there is an implicit condition ("If you are a student ..."). Put it first.

- Put instructions in the order in which they must be completed.[1]

Break up walls of words. Break the information into short, manageable pieces. These breaks should not be arbitrary, but should help readers understand the information better by creating a logical structure. Shorter sections and paragraphs also create white space, and make the content seem more approachable.

Use lots of (useful) headings. Create meaningful, useful headings for each section. Good headings communicate the structure and key points of your content, helping readers scan to the right section. Headings can be questions ("Why do we use headings?"), statements ("Headings help guide readers"), or topics ("Good headings").

Talk to your readers. It's OK to get personal and talk directly, using "you." Or you can use the imperative to tell readers what they have to do. Talking directly to your readers makes a better conversation.

---

1 Steehouder, M. F. and Jansen, C. J. M. (1996) "The Sequential Order of Instructions: Impact on Text Quality" in Proceedings of the 43rd Annual Conference of the Society for Technical Communication.

Make your writing active. Write in the active voice (most of the time). Passive sentences sound weak, and don't make a good call to action. Active writing includes an *actor*: "You ordered this product on March 19, 2012" is stronger than "The product was ordered on March 19, 2012."

Put the action in the verbs. Use simple, clear verbs instead of hiding the action in a noun. Write "Pay by credit card" not "Make a payment using a credit card." (In this example, "pay" is an active verb, while "payment" is a noun form that uses the weaker "make" as the verb.) Putting the action in the verb uses fewer words, emphasizes the action, and is just plain clearer.

Use bulleted lists (where appropriate). When you have a list of items, or a collection of conditions, use bulleted lists or tables to make it easy to see how many different things you are talking about.

Support users through their tasks

If you stay focused on the purpose of the site, it's a lot easier to decide what to say. Whether you are writing content for an informational website or for a complex, interactive application, the goal of your words is to support people in meeting their goals. The menus, titles, links, field labels, prompts, and instructions all have to work together, and they have to work with everything else about the product design.

When you organize the information from the reader's perspective and talk directly to the readers, supporting users is easier. For example, Figure 8.1 shows the result of a self-assessment quiz to help individuals understand their risk of colon cancer. This content doesn't lecture or try to teach too much medical science. Instead, it provides clear information and possible actions to address the users' real goal: finding out how they can stay healthy.

- The page starts with the simplest possible statement of the results, that "Compared to a typical woman your age, your risk is much below average."
- The next paragraph explains what this risk means, tailored to the actual results.
- The results are shown graphically, reinforcing the meaning, with links to more detailed information.
- Even the results are interactive, letting users see how much they can affect their own level of risk.
- The page ends with a list of the things the user is doing right, encouraging good habits.

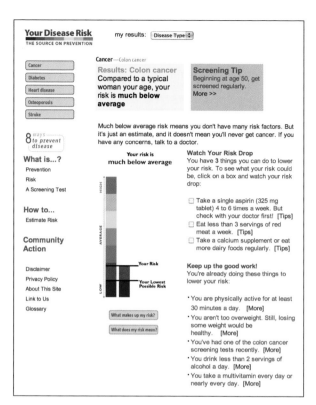

FIGURE 8.1

This e-health tool presents the results of a self-assessment in a way that helps everyone—even people with lower health literacy— understand what their risk is, and what they can do about it. (www. yourdiseaserisk.wustl. edu/hccpquiz.pl)

Structure the whole page for scanning and understanding

Users don't think about "the content" separately from "the page," so you shouldn't either. Structure the page, content, and presentation so that they all work together to communicate clearly. Here are three basic guidelines to use to support scanning:

- Break up walls of words.
- Use (correctly tagged) bullets for lists.
- Use lots of (useful) headings.

Another way to structure content to support scanning is by considering how much information readers need at each place, and structuring information to lead from simpler to more detailed explanations. This "layering" of information can be as simple as creating a good organization within a single page, or by using "progressive disclosure," to allow users to reveal more detailed information. (See Chapter 10, "Universal Usability," *Design for exploration and discovery* for more information on progressive disclosure.) Done correctly, this approach meets the needs of visual and verbal learners, people who don't read well, those who prefer numbers, and people using screen readers.

Figure 8.2 from the Career One Stop site is a good example of how to structure information. The chart and associated data shows that people with more education both earn more and are less likely to be unemployed.

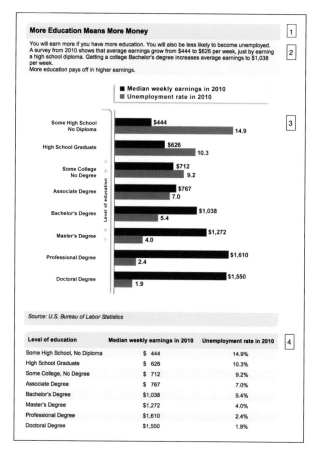

FIGURE 8.2
Career One Stop, a website for job seekers, includes charts showing what makes a difference in employment and earnings. (Numbers in the image match the list below.) (www.careerinfonet.org/finaidadvisor/earnings.aspx?nodeid=21)

To make the findings clear and comprehensible, the page has:

1. **A meaningful title** that sums up the point the authors want to make: "More education means more money" (instead of "Earnings and Education").

2. **A short summary paragraph** that adds a little more detail, but still aims to make the point in a very concise way. It says, "You will earn more if you have more education. You will also be less likely to

become unemployed. A survey from 2010 shows that average earnings grow from $454 to $626 per week, just by earning a high school diploma. Getting a college Bachelor's degree increases average earnings to $1,025 per week. More education pays off in higher earnings."

3. **The data in a graph.** The graph is formatted to make it easier to add labels, putting the data into numbers, as well as showing it visually. For screen readers, the alternative (alt) text for the image says "Chart of data table below." The colors of the bars work in grayscale and for people with color blindness.

4. **The data is presented in a table,** so that people who prefer numbers or who cannot see the chart easily have access to the information.

In addition to structuring the information visually, make sure that it is structured semantically with good markup. Semantic markup allows people using assistive technology to scan, for example, document headings and jump quickly to different sections. (We discuss semantic markup in more detail in Chapter 4, "Solid Structure," *Use semantic markup for content.*)

- Use heading tags, nested in the correct order for headings.
- Use tags for bulleted and numbered lists.
- Use tables appropriately, with tags for header rows

Write sentences and paragraphs for easy scanning

You can also structure sentences for easy scanning by putting keywords at the beginning of the sentence. Visual readers can easily scan down the page. There are two common patterns for scanning a page visually (shown in Figure 8.3). When scanning a page, the eyes move down the page in an "F" pattern, reading a few words at the beginning of each line or paragraph. In contrast, in steady reading, the eye tracks across each line, reading each word. People using screen readers can also scan, because they don't have to listen to the whole sentence, link, or bullet to find the information they want.

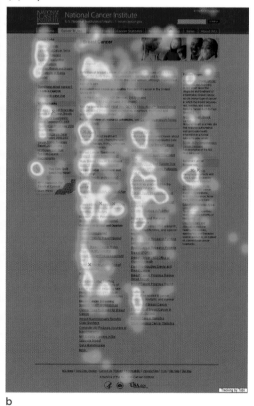

FIGURE 8.3

Eye tracking heatmaps show two reading patterns. (a) Steady reading pattern. (b) F-pattern.

a

b

Reading is hard for me.

It takes me a long time to read things. My teachers want me to work on my vocabulary, but I'd rather just find easier pages to read. Instructions are really hard for me. Going back and forth between the instructions and what I have to do is very, very distracting. Sometimes I'm trying to read, and I get interested in something on the side of the page and forget what I'm supposed to be doing. But sometimes, I get really involved in what I'm reading and keep going, even after I found what I'm looking up. It can take me a very long time to do any homework assignment. I wish websites were more like books, with nothing to distract me.

Trevor

Write helpful links

Make link text meaningful. The text of a link should clearly and unambiguously tell the reader where the link points.

- If the link points to anything other than another web page—to PDF, Word, or other files—say so in the text of the link ("My Presentation (PPT)"). Some sites suggest adding the file size as well ("My Presentation (PDF 645Kb)").

- If you have a list of similar links, put the most meaningful word at the beginning of the link text. This makes it easier for users to scan the list quickly (either visually or in audio). See Figure 8.4.

Combining links and images. It's common to combine several elements, such as an image and text, to provide a "teaser" link to the full article. When each element is coded individually, the result is multiple links to the same destination, which can be confusing and tiresome to, for example, screen reader and keyboard users who tab from link to link. The best approach is to combine the elements into one descriptive link to provide a single point of access (see Figure 8.5).

"Read more" links. Watch out for links that repeat the same word over and over. It's tempting to add a link that says "Read more ..." at the end of a summary, but it's just as easy, and clearer, to link the headline instead. Your goal is to make the linked text be clear enough for users to understand it, even out of context. Screen reader users will often review a list of the links on the page even before reading the page to get an overview of the content.

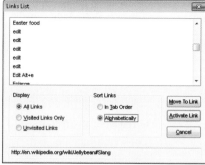

FIGURE 8.4

In a usability study, Mary Frances Theofanos and Ginny Redish found that blind users "scan with their ears," listening to just enough to decide whether to listen further. Scanning can be difficult when links are repetitive and not descriptive, as illustrated in this JAWS Links List. (Read about the study: Theofanos, M. F. and Redish, J. C., 2003, "Guidelines for Accessible and Usable Websites: Observing Users Who Work with Screen Readers," *Interactions*, X (6), November–December, 38–51. (www.redish.net/content/papers/interactions.html)

The title attribute. When writing links, don't be tempted to rely on the title attribute to make sense of the link. Browsers and screen readers each handle title differently, so the attribute is not a reliable way to add information to a link. More importantly, don't provide the same information in the title and link text, or in the title and alt text for an image.

Many content management tools prompt users to add a title when creating a link and adding an image. The title attribute should be unnecessary, with well-written links and appropriate image alt text. Unfortunately, CMS users often repeat the link or alt text in the title field. As a result, the web is cluttered with repetitive tooltips.

FIGURE 8.5

In the first example, screen reader users will hear the link to "Mercado de San Miguel" only once because the image has null alt text. In the second example, the title attribute causes a tooltip to appear over the link, and may mean the name of the park is repeated.

Use language your audience is familiar with or provide definitions

Writing for your audience means using terminology *your audience* understands. We've emphasized "your audience" because we are not suggesting that all content needs to be reduced to one-syllable words. Plain, accessible language is language that fits the context and the audience.

On the web, it can be hard to know exactly who is reading your content, or how familiar they are with the subject, so it's safest not to make any assumptions. Provide definitions for unusual words, words used in a specific way in your context, and for all abbreviations. You can use layering to let users drill down to the level of information they need:

- **Define terms in the text.** Explain a concept and then introduce the technical term.

- **Use a glossary.** Quick definitions can be presented in a smaller second window, allowing users to easily return to the same spot in the main page. Be sure to give the window a meaningful title.

- **Link to more detailed information.** Keep definitions short by linking to a full page if there are more details that users might find useful.

In addition to terminology, "language" can mean a language like Spanish or English. Help screen readers pronounce words correctly by marking the language in the code. You can set the language for the whole page, or if there is more than one language on a page, you can add codes to mark changes from one language to another.

Provide plain language summaries of complex content

If it is not possible to write in sufficiently plain language, provide an alternative version or a simplified summary. Not only will it help make your site more accessible for people with reading disabilities, but you might also find that it helps rushed readers as well. For example, Lainey Feingold's website contains articles about her legal work for accessibility rights. All of the pages include simplified summaries that describe the main point on the page (shown in Figure 8.6).

When including simplified summaries, consider how they will be placed on the page early in the design process. They need to be easy to find for people who need them, but not presented in a way that is intrusive or confusing.

> **Simplified Summary:** This is a post about cancer related information available to people who are blind and visually impaired. Call the American Cancer Society toll-free at 1-800-227-2345 to order certain publications in Braille, Large Print, audio CD, mp3 file or in accessible PDF. [Back to post about accessible information at the American Cancer Society .]

FIGURE 8.6

This summary is from a page that describes an agreement with the American Cancer Society. http://lflegal.com/2011/03/acs-info/

The U.S. National Cancer Institute Fact Sheets on cancer topics include a box with Key Points at the top of the page (see Figure 8.7). These summaries are useful for patients and other members of the general public because some of the topics include detailed medical information. The NCI web content team worried that the summaries might be a barrier for health professionals by suggesting that the entire page is as simple as the key points. But when they tested the design, professionals said they recognized that "boxes like those" were simple summaries for patients, and just skipped over them.

Key Points

- Cancer that starts in the bone is uncommon.
- Pain is the most common symptom of bone cancer.
- Surgery is the usual treatment for bone cancer.
- With modern surgical techniques, 9 out of 10 people who have bone cancer in an arm or leg may not need amputation.
- Because bone cancer can come back after treatment, regular follow-up visits are important.
- People with bone cancer are encouraged to enroll in clinical trials (research studies) that explore new treatments.

FIGURE 8.7

NCI's cancer fact sheets start with a summary of the key points that everyone needs to know. (www.cancer.gov/cancertopics/factsheet/Sites-Types/bone)

Alt text for online editions is included here so that it's handy. It does not appear on the printed page, and is not bulleted.

Don't rely on readability formulas

Many people have the misconception that plain language can be defined by testing the content for reading level or grade level. Readability formulas may seem like a way to define clear writing, but they are not a very good way of evaluating plain language. The reason is simple: these formulas work by counting syllables in words and words in sentences, and those counts have very little to do with whether the information is readable. They also ignore an important part of the definition of plain

Easy Read is a program in the U.K. aimed at providing information that people with learning disabilities need to know—government policies and benefits.

Their guidelines include how the text is both written and presented to make information clear for people who do not read well. You can download the complete set of guidelines, but the most important concepts are drawn from principles for both plain language and clean presentation:

- Present each main idea in both words and pictures. Each picture should clearly illustrate a single idea, and not be used for more than one idea in a document.
- Break up text to highlight important points with bullets, boxed text, and bold text.
- Highlight difficult words the first time they appear and put an explanation immediately after the word.
- Use a simple sans-serif font at a minimum of 16 points.
- Use color to draw attention.
- Use a lot of white space, both around the text and between lines.

Easy Read is not universal design but an alternative version. However, creating an Easy Read version is a good way to think about the most important points being communicated. One way to think about Easy Read is that it is a concise summary of the content.

Figure 8.8 shows two versions of a document—the text version and the Easy Read version—side-by-side. The same questions are presented in both plain language and an Easy Read simplified version.

Questions for Public Consultation

5. The four questions on which we seek your views are:
   (1) do you think we need a UK Bill of Rights?
   If so,
   (2) what do you think a UK Bill of Rights should contain?
   (3) how do you think it should apply to the UK as a whole, including its four component countries of England, Northern Ireland, Scotland and Wales?
   (4) having regard to our terms of reference, are there any other views which you would like to put forward at this stage?

6. The remainder of this paper sets out background to these questions, and is put forward as an aid to understanding. It aims to describe the current position in purely factual terms.

We want to know:

Question 1
Do you think we need a Bill of Rights in the UK?

If you do,

Question 2
What should be in the Bill of Rights?

Question 3
If we had a Bill of Rights in the UK, should it be the same or different in the different parts of the UK such as in England, Northern Ireland, Scotland or Wales?

Question 4
Is there anything else you want to tell us about our work?

FIGURE 8.8

For more about Easy Read: www.dh.gov.uk/en/Publicationsandstatistics/Publications/PublicationsPolicyAndGuidance/DH_12194

language: that the content is written for the readers. Formulas can let you know if text is not plain, but they cannot tell you if you have written in a way that is useful for the audience.

Readability formulas do have one use: as an early warning system. They can be a way of checking whether you have too many long sentences or multi-syllable words, but not much more.

In her talk, "The Right to Understand," at TEDxO'Porto, Sandra Fisher-Martins says that the percentage of people who read at different levels of literacy made her realize that not being able to read is a kind of disability. In Portugal, 50% of people read at the lowest level (shown as figures in red in Figure 8.9) compared to just 5% in Sweden.

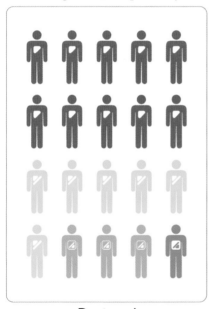
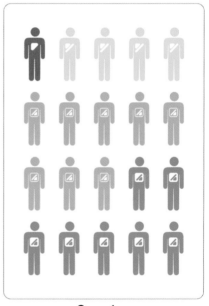

Portugal   Sweden

FIGURE 8.9

A visual presentation of literacy levels in Portugal (left) and Sweden (right). See "A Symbol Language for Color" in Chapter 9, "Accessible Media," for a description of the ColorAdd symbols used in this presentation. (www.youtube.com/watch?v=tP2yOvU7EG8)

Usability test your content

Too often, we test the structure and templates for a site, but don't test with real content, even though the "content" is often the real reason visitors come to the site. Including real content from the beginning of a project, from the first wireframe, has several benefits.

- The content team—content strategists, authors, multimedia producers, and other contributors—has an active part in the project from the beginning. They can provide samples of all types of information, so the overall product design fits the content well, and vice versa.

- Test content early to check the "voice" of the site, whether the terminology is meaningful, and whether there is the right amount of detail.

- Users can react to the site in a more natural way. Greeking[2] text (blocks of text with words like "lorem ipsum" instead of real content) is often confusing to test participants.

Who Is Responsible for Plain Language?

Plain language is content, so content strategists, authors, editors, and other contributors have the primary responsibility for making sure that all of the information on the site is written using language appropriate for the audience.

- Formatted for scanning, using headings and breaking up walls of words.

- Formatted with semantic markup.

Some aspects of plain language are implemented in design and code. Those teams support the content authors with clear presentation and structural support for plain language. Remember that there is a lot of language in the interface: in the form of button labels, navigational links, section titles, and more. Those need to be written in plain language, no matter who writes them.

In addition, features that support plain language need to be designed and built into the product. This starts with a stylesheet that supports clean presentation and semantic coding that fits the content.

---

2 The text comes from an old text by Cicero. Using those words as placeholder text goes back to the beginning of printing. It's called "Greeking" the text because you aren't expected to understand it. **www.lipsum.com/**

WCAG 2.0 and Plain Language

The guidelines for Plain Language map to the following WCAG 2.0 requirements.

A site with plain language is **Understandable**, written for the audience.

A site with plain language meets the guidelines:

- **3.1 Readable:** Make text content readable and understandable (Guideline).

The requirements for plain language are:

- **2.4.6 and 2.4.10 Headings and Labels:** Headings and labels describe topic or purpose (Level AA) and are used to organize the content (Level AAA).
- **2.4.4 and 2.4.9 Link Purpose:** The purpose of each link can be determined from the link text alone (Level AAA) or from the link text together with the context (Level A).
- **3.1.1 and 3.1.2 Language of Page/Parts:** The default human language of each web page (Level A) or of each passage or phrase in the content (Level AA) is defined in code.
- **3.1.3 Unusual Words:** The site includes definitions of words or phrases used in an unusual or restricted way, including idioms and jargon (Level AAA).
- **3.1.4 Abbreviations:** The meaning of abbreviations is available (Level AAA).
- **3.1.6 Pronunciation:** There is a way to identify the pronunciation of words where the meaning of the words is ambiguous without the pronunciation (Level AAA).
- **3.3.2 Labels or Instructions:** Labels or instructions are provided when content requires user input (Level A).
- **3.3.5 Help:** Context-sensitive help is available (Level AAA).
- **3.1.5 Reading Level:** When text requires reading ability beyond a lower secondary education level, a simplified summary or version is available (Level AAA).

The full text of the WCAG 2.0 requirements can be found in Appendix B.

Summary

Plain language involves accessibility for content, helping everyone read more accurately and efficiently. Writing in plain language does not mean "dumbing down" the information. It means writing for the audience, using words and concepts they will understand.

Plain language and clean presentation work together—both rely on structuring the content well and designing or writing to support comprehension. Well-written headings support users in scanning the page, whether they are reading visually or through the semantic structure of the page.

Content at the word, sentence, paragraph, and page level can all be made easier to read by following guidelines for plain language to write clearly and in a way that's easy to scan.

Be sure to test for plain language through usability testing, not through reading level metrics, which do little more than count words and syllables.

Ginny Redish has been helping people write clearly for all of her career. She does research and analysis to understand what's hard about reading and writing, and follows up with guidelines that people can use to make reading and writing easier.

In our experience, language and content often get less attention than other elements in design projects. We wanted to learn from Ginny how to make language more of a priority.

Plain language is important for accessibility.

Plain language is all about accessibility—making information understandable for everyone. "It's not a matter of dumbing down. It's a matter of meeting people where they are and saving people's time."

Plain language is particularly important on "functional websites," where people go to get information and accomplish tasks. The goal is that "people can *find* what they need, *understand* what they find, and *use* that to accomplish whatever it is they need to accomplish." Providing that experience to the broadest range of users is the goal of universal plain language.

We all have difficulty reading at some time or another, for physical or cognitive reasons, or when encountering an unknown topic or language. "Even people who read with high literacy sometimes have problems reading—when they are under stress, or when it's an unfamiliar topic." In the end, "plain language is valuable—even necessary—to just about everybody."

When you use plain language, "people can *find* what they need, *understand* what they find, and *use* that to accomplish whatever it is they need to accomplish." And *plain* does not mean *dull*. "It's not a matter of dumbing down. It's a matter of meeting people where they are and saving people's time. People don't come to functional websites to waste time. They are very busy with other parts of their lives. They need to be able to find, understand, and use the information in the time and effort that they think it's worth."

Can one source of information work for everyone? "If you write your main content in plain language, you are going to reach a wide range of your audience," but there are times when "different audiences need different content." The decision to create different content should be undertaken deliberately and with caution because alternate versions are frequently neglected. "Separate but equal is never equal."

profile continues on next page

Design projects need content people.

The need to make decisions about the right content for the audience illustrates the importance of having a content strategist on the design team. Typically, teams don't consider content until the very end of the design process, and then content providers scramble to replace "lorem ipsum" placeholder text with actual information. And more often than not, the people producing the words are not trained as writers, never mind in the techniques of plain language. As a result, the very thing people come for—information—is often the most poorly implemented part of a design.

> *People who come to websites don't come to navigate. They don't come to admire your design. Obviously, the design and navigation are potential barriers, and they have to be good so as not to be barriers. But what people come for is the content, and the content is both information design and language. Understanding its importance and making content an integral part of the process is critical. Plain language must be part of the design process from the start.*

Implementing plain language in the design process requires content people, real content, and a commitment to conversation. Every project should have professional content people on the team from the start—people who know how to write "clearly and conversationally."

Secondly, real content for the site should be in place from the very beginning of the process, and tested and modified throughout the process, along with other design elements. Ginny urges, "No more lorem ipsum!"

Finally, the design team should adopt a philosophy based on engaging in a conversation. "Your content strategy can't be a one-way spewing of information. It needs to be answering site visitors' questions. And if you think about content as a conversation, you are much more likely to write in plain language."

Making a commitment to plain language and integrating plain language into the design process improve accessibility in an integrated and holistic way. No one is adversely affected by language that is clear and to the point—in fact, everyone understands better. Working toward the goal of universal plain language is one of the best ways to improve the user experience for everyone.

> *One of the most interesting aspects of the ADA movement has been how often something created to meet the needs of a special group of people has turned out to be useful for everybody. Plain language is the same. People think of plain language for a low literacy audience. But when we simplify and clarify for a low literacy audience, high literacy people benefit just as much and sometimes even more.*

CHAPTER 9

Accessible Media: Supports All Senses

Closed Captions

Public screens, in airports or on the side of a building, are examples of the many places where closed captions allow everyone to watch televisions without sound—even when driving by.

Perhaps the most common accessible medium is closed captioning for television programs. Closed captioning was developed to make programs accessible to people who are deaf or hard of hearing. Television screens in airports, shops, gyms, and bars often play with the sound turned off and captions turned on.

In many countries, closed captions are required by law or provided routinely on most television programs. In the U.S., for example, the first closed captioning service started in the 1980s and is now part of virtually all broadcast and cable television programming. It was invented by PBS, NIST, and ABC-TV, earning a technology Emmy Award. The first TV show with closed captions was an episode of *The Mod Squad* (open captions were available even earlier, starting in 1972 on *Julia Child's French Chef*). The 21st Century Communications and Video Accessibility Act of 2010 requires captions for TV programs shown on the Internet, if they were previously captioned, but does not cover programs shown only online.

In most of the principles we have discussed so far, making websites or apps accessible does not require much beyond good design or development practice. You may have to learn a few new techniques, but once you do, accessibility becomes second nature.

Creating accessible media is different. With media, you have to do something extra to make it accessible—captions for the sounds in audio or video and descriptions for visual images. These alternatives must be built into the media or site explicitly because images, audio, and video do not contain information in a form that allows current technology to read them directly.

How Accessible Media Supports Accessibility

Making media accessible is critical for a simple reason: without alternatives, the information in images, audio, and video is completely hidden from some people. This creates an absolute barrier to understanding the content and a generally frustrating experience for people who can't access the information.

Although there are different techniques for making images and motion media accessible, the basic principle is the same: provide alternatives so that they work for all senses.

With accessible media, **people can understand and use information contained in media, such as images, audio, video, animation, and presentations.**

- **Information in media is available to everyone.** You can't see the experience of time-based media here, on a printed page, but you can look at the difference accessible images make in a web experience. By providing alternative text, the information is available to both people who can see the images and people who need text that can be read out loud (see Figure 9.1). Similarly, captions and video description make video accessible to people who cannot hear the audio.

- **People have alternative ways to consume information.** Making media accessible helps people with disabilities, but it also helps people in situations that limit their use of sight or hearing: noisy spaces, places where they cannot make noise without disturbing others, low light, or bright light. Another consideration is that we all use our senses in different ways. Some people prefer to learn through visual concepts and presentations, some prefer to learn by reading, and others by doing. Building in options with media alternatives helps everyone.

a   b

FIGURE 9.1

Without alternative text for images, information can disappear for screen readers or people using a text view. With alternatives, they can have an equivalent experience. (a) This is the default view of the National Park Service site. (b) With images turned off, the content images are replaced with alternative text.

Maria

When I hear *and* see it, health information makes more sense.

My new phone is so good for my work. I don't have to carry around so much paper because I can pull it up from my bookmarks. I even tried watching one of my health educator's videos, but the captions were hard to read on the phone. Those captions are very nice. I can see the words spelled out while I hear them, so I learn how to spell them, too. It's also nice to give videos to my clients. Sometimes they don't read English well, but they can listen OK.

How to Design for Accessible Media

The simplest guideline for thinking about universal design for any kind of media is to use multiple communication methods. Most importantly, don't rely on just one sense, such as sight, color perception, or hearing.

Don't use *only* color to communicate meaning

One of the first rules of accessibility that many people learn is "not by color alone." This doesn't mean not to use color at all—far from it. Color is an important part of design. It just means you must use redundant cues of shape, position, or text to reinforce the meaning (see Table 9.1).

This guideline applies to symbols, graphs and charts, and the color combinations for text and the background in any medium, including images, presentations, animations, and information in a video.

TABLE 9.1 COLOR + ANOTHER CUE = MEANING FOR ALL

Ways to create meaning	Image with color and in shades of gray				
These symbols are meaningless without color. In this example, green and red diamonds show whether the product has a feature or not.		Fruit?			Fruit?
	Apples	◆	Apples		◆
	Kittens	◆	Kittens		◆
	Oranges	◆	Oranges		◆
	Puppies	◆	Puppies		◆
Use position. In this example, the symbols are placed in columns under the headings "Yes" and "No."		Yes	No	Yes	No
	Apples	◆		Apples	◆
	Kittens		◆	Kittens	◆
	Oranges	◆		Oranges	◆
	Puppies		◆	Puppies	◆
Use different symbols. In this example, the symbol for Yes is a green check, and the symbol for No is a red "x." If these symbols are images, they can also have alt text that spells out the meaning.		Yes	No	Yes	No
	Apples	✔		Apples	✔
	Kittens		✘	Kittens	✘
	Oranges	✔		Oranges	✔
	Puppies		✘	Puppies	✘
Use words. In this example, the word Yes is green, and the word No is red.		Fruit?			Fruit?
	Apples	Yes	Apples		Yes
	Kittens	No	Kittens		No
	Oranges	Yes	Oranges		Yes
	Puppies	No	Puppies		No

Designer Miguel Neiva realized that as color becomes a more and more critical part of communication, the 350 million people (including 10% of men) with some type of color blindness are easily left out.

His solution is a symbol language called ColorADD Color Identification System, shown in Figure 9.2, in which shape can communicate color. It works by using a small set of symbols that start with blue, yellow, and red, and mix those symbols to show the major colors on the spectrum.

His vision is that these symbols could appear on clothing labels or any product in a color, but also for healthcare uses like safety labels, and color-coded patient wrist bands that patients wear.

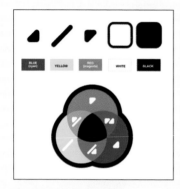 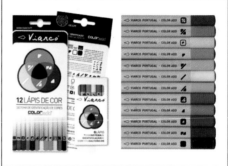

FIGURE 9.2

ColorADD Color Identification System symbols on a set of colored pencils show how they can work in practice. (www.coloradd.net)

Provide instructions without relying on visual cues

When communicating information through color, remember that the need to provide information for all senses applies to instructions, too. If you tell someone who can't see color to "click on the green button," or "fill in the fields highlighted in yellow," those instructions are just not useful. Similarly, the information that a heading is on the right side of the page is not useful for someone using an audio interface.

Don't use descriptions of the color, shape, or location of an element as the only cues for how to find it. Name elements in the interface with the text label, so that users can identify and locate them accurately, no matter how they are accessing the page.

Describe the content or meaning of images

When you put an image on a page, you do so for a reason. The image communicates visually, so you also need to communicate the same information as text. You do this by using "alternative text," or alt text, inside the image tag. Browsers use the alt text in place of images that are not displayed or are not accessible to the user.

For example, when a screen reader finds an image, it announces that it has found an image, and reads any alt text. In this way, the alt text replaces the image for non-visual access.

FIGURE 9.3
Depending on the purpose of this image in the page, the alt text might read: "Red fox" or "Red fox at Sachuest Point National Wildlife Refuge," or "A red fox, standing alone on a pile of rocks, looks back at the camera."

To write useful alt text, you must decide how best to describe the image to communicate an equivalent meaning. To do this well, you have to think about the purpose of the image and its context of use (see Figure 9.3), including whether there is information in the image that is not repeated elsewhere in the content. When alt text is too long, or has more information than is really meaningful, it can be distracting instead of adding to the experience.

The only absolute rule for writing alternative text is that **every image must include an alt attribute.**

The following guidelines will help you write useful, meaningful alt text.

Repeat words from the image. If an image contains text in graphical form, repeat the same words in the alt text. Unless there is meaningful information in how the text is presented, don't add words describing the color or other decorative elements. (See Figure 9.4.)

FIGURE 9.4

The alternative text for this image should repeat the words in the image: "Webcast: Applying 21st Century Toxicology to Green Chemical and Material Design, September 20-21, 2011."

The best practice is to use HTML text whenever possible, rather than text in a graphical format, as text in an image cannot be read by software. (See Chapter 4, "Solid Structure," *Code content to be machine-readable*.)

Use blank alt text for decorative images. If an image is used purely for decoration, don't clutter the interface by describing it. For these images, include the alt attribute, but leave its value blank: alt="" (that is, 'quote quote', with no space in between). This is called "null alt text." It allows software to distinguish between images that are purely decorative and should not be communicated to the user and images where no one bothered to provide alt text. (See Figure 9.5.)

This category of images includes:

- Icons that duplicate information already in the text
- Graphical bullets
- Decorative separators or icons that only have meaning in the visual layout

```
<a href="contact.html"><img src="email-icon.gif" alt="" />Email</a>
```

FIGURE 9.5

Icons that reinforce links should have null alt text since their purpose is purely visual. With null alt text, screen reader software will skip over the images and read only the links.

Describe images in a meaningful way. For images that add visual interest to a headline or paragraph of text, you can choose to:

- Provide a very brief description of the content of the image, in order to communicate the impact of the image in words.

- Use null alt text if the image is generic rather than an illustration of a specific person, event, or place, but only if there is no extra information communicated by the picture.

Identify the target of a link. If the image is a link, write the alt text as though you were writing link text, describing the link destination as opposed to the image.

It's particularly important to supply alt text when an image is used as a link. Without alt text, screen readers have nothing other than the image file name to describe the link, which in most cases is not that descriptive. If a linked image is associated with a text link, you can use null alt text so the user won't have to hear the same words twice.

Don't use a file name or other technical information. This might be helpful to you as the author, but it's not very helpful or a good experience for the user. Some web authoring programs automatically insert file names into the alt text. These images will pass a test for alternative text, meeting the letter of the rule, but not the spirit.

Only use background images for decorative effects. Background images can provide a visual effect like color or texture to the whole page. Background images added using CSS do not have alternative text available to a screen reader. If the image is purely decorative, the missing alt text is not a problem, but if the image adds meaning, be sure that any information is duplicated in HTML text content.

Beyond these basics, you have to make decisions about how to write the most usable and meaningful alt text based on the context and what is in the caption. The real test of good alternative text for images is whether the page communicates just as well, providing equivalent information and an equally good experience, both with and without seeing the images.

Provide captions and descriptions for video

Captions are the words that appear at the bottom of a video screen, providing a text version of the audio track. They always include the words spoken in the video. They should also include all significant audio content, such as a phone ringing, horns honking, music playing, or other sounds that are important in understanding the meaning.

One of the hot debates as we write this book is what happens with detailed images, such as diagrams, illustrations, and charts, that need more description. In HTML 4.01, an image tag can contain a "longdesc" attribute to provide a link to a page containing a long description of the image. Unfortunately, the attribute has been implemented erratically and is therefore not used much. Images needing more lengthy descriptions are often described in alt text or not at all.

Look at Figure 9.6 and see what you think. In this image, the long description is contained in the alt text, providing details about what is shown in the image: "Anatomy of the pancreas; drawing shows the pancreas, stomach, spleen, liver, gallbladder, bile ducts, colon, and small intestine. An inset shows the head, body, and tail of the pancreas. The bile duct and pancreatic duct are also shown."

The caption describes the purpose of the image: "Anatomy of the pancreas. The pancreas has three areas: head, body, and tail. It is found in the abdomen near the stomach, intestines, and other organs."

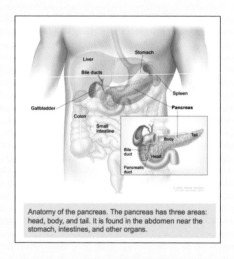

FIGURE 9.6

A medical illustration showing the anatomy of the pancreas.

Anatomy of the pancreas. The pancreas has three areas: head, body, and tail. It is found in the abdomen near the stomach, intestines, and other organs.

The "longdesc" attribute was dropped from the HTML5 specification, and since then there has been much debate over how to replace it. Steve Faulkner, profiled in Chapter 6, "Helpful Wayfinding," has been in the middle of the work to find a solution, so that it's easy to provide links between images and long descriptions.

While there's still some debate over whether "longdesc" should be part of the spec, it's not a safe option for providing long descriptions. Steve offers practical guidance on ways to provide text alternatives in "HTML5: Techniques for Providing Useful Text Alternatives" (http://dev.w3.org/html5/alt-techniques/developer.html).

Steven

Without captions, it's meaningless to me.

I love that there is so much visual information on the web, but when it comes to videos, why can't people take the time to include me? For example, I was trying to learn how to use a new application, and the only instructions were in a screencast. I could sort of follow what they were doing, but when someone interpreted for me, I found out that I misunderstood an important point. It makes me so frustrated. I'm good at what I do, and don't like being left out or having to ask someone to interpret information for me.

Video description (also called *audio description* or *described video*) uses the natural pauses in dialogue to add narrative that translates visual information into descriptive text, so that blind members of an audience have access to this information (see Table 9.2). On the web, audio description may be provided in several ways:

- In the main audio track.
- In a separate audio track. This allows users to choose to listen to this track, but does not work in all media players.
- In a separate text file or added to an audio transcript.

Captions are added to a video through a text file that contains both the text of the caption and the time codes to tell the video player when to display the text. Figure 9.7 shows a sample of a caption file.

```
0:00:13.369,0:00:15.700
If you wish to increase the playback speed,

0:00:15.700,0:00:22.700
press the pound key at any time. Press the
star key to decrease the playback speed.
```

FIGURE 9.7
There are several different caption formats. This is a sample of one caption format that YouTube supports, SubViewer (SBV). Other popular formats are SpokenMedia's (WRD) and SubRip (SRT).

TABLE 9.2 DEFINITIONS : ALTERNATIVES FOR AUDIO AND VIDEO

Subtitles	Translations to a second language.
	Subtitles can also be used for audio that is difficult to hear because of background noise, accents, or muffled speech.
Captions	A synchronized display of the transcript where the text and spoken word are in the same language.
	Captions can be open or closed:
	• Open captions are burned into the video, so that everyone sees them.
	• Closed captions can be turned on or off, so that they are only seen when needed.
Audio Description/ Video Description	Not just what's said, but a more complete description of the action, filling in gaps missing for people who cannot hear the audio track, or see the visuals.
	• Adds captions for non-speech audio, such as music, phone rings, explosions, etc.
	• Describes action not spoken in dialogue. For example, if there is a loud explosion, the description would include what blew up, if it is not obvious from the context.

The process for creating captions starts with a transcript. Depending on how the multimedia was created, you may already have a script that you can use as the starting point.

- **A complete script.** Videos for e-learning, screencasts, or that use an announcer or actors often have a complete script that is an effective transcript.

- **A rough script.** Speeches or informal presentations' videos might have rough speaker notes that can be a good start on a full transcript.

- **No script.** Interviews or journalistic videos often have no script at all, so they have to be completely transcribed.

You then add time-codes, typically using a tool (like the ones shown in Figure 9.8) to help synchronize the text with the video.

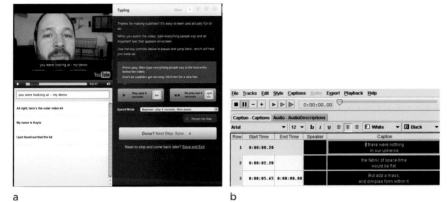

a   b

FIGURE 9.8

(a) The Amara (universalsubtitles.org) editor makes it easy to see
how the captions will synchronize with the video. Amara allows you
to create captions for any video, even if you don't have access to it on
the server. (b) The Magpie captions editor from NCAM (ncam.wgbh.
org) focuses on displaying the timecodes and associated captions in
a compact and easy-to-read form.

As speech-to-text technology has improved, there are now options for
automatic captions. YouTube, for example, will attempt to create captions using automatic speech recognition (ASR). The results are often
not very good unless the audio is clear and the speech distinct. However,
they can be a good way to get started: the file provides the time stamps,
and you can edit the automatically created captions to correct the text.

Format captions to enhance meaning

With such a restricted format, you might not think about using text
styling to enhance meaning (see Table 9.3). Subtle uses of spacing, punc-
tuation, and line breaks can help users read the captions more easily.

Caption authors can reserve one, two, or more lines of text for captions. Long captions will wrap automatically, but it's a good practice to
check to be sure that the text is not so long that it's hard to read, that the
breaks between captions match the phrasing of the spoken text, and that
there is enough contrast between the caption text and the background.

TABLE 9.3 STYLE CONVENTIONS FOR CAPTIONS

Line breaks	Put line breaks and breaks between captions in logical places in the phrasing. This makes it easier to follow the meaning of the words.
	
	`The quick brown fox`
	
	`jumps over the lazy dog`

Periods	Put a period at the end of sentences. Start the new sentence with a new caption.
	
	`Welcome to the Twitter translation center.`
	
	`In order to help make Twitter available`
	
	`to everyone in the world,`

Non-verbal sounds	Put non-verbal sounds in parentheses or square brackets. Consider naming the title of the song, if it is important to the meaning.
	
	`(dog barking)`
	
	`[phone ringing ...]`
	
	`[music playing: Title of Song]`
	
	`Hang on a sec. (music stops)`

Speaker identification	If the visual image does not show the person who is speaking, or if the audio cuts between two speakers, identify the person speaking.
	
	• Use a colon after the name
	
	• Add angle brackets where a new voice starts
	
	• Use ALL CAPS for the name (if the caption text is in mixed case) or vice versa
	
	If the video identifies the speaker at the bottom of the screen, consider including the title or description, because it may be obscured by the caption.
	
	Examples of four ways to identify speakers or indicate when the speaker changes.
	
	`PRESIDENT OBAMA: We'll take one more question.`
	
	`>> Can you tell us when this will take effect?`
	
	`JAMES SMITH, Hometown Press: I'D LIKE TO KNOW`
	
	`JAMES SMITH: What time is it? MARY: Almost 3:00.`

Sean Zdenek, a technical communications professor at Texas Tech University, has been exploring the rhetoric of captions—that is, the art of discourse and communication applied to closed captions. He has tackled issues like how to communicate humor, drunken speech, accents, irony, and the meaning of sounds.

He suggests using parentheticals (which he calls "manner captions") to tell readers how the words are pronounced. Think about how much these brief descriptions add to your understanding of the story.

```
(WHISPERS) Don't go!
(IN SILLY VOICE) And I'll tell you what the first thing
(SCORNFULLY) their deity
(drunken slurring) It's a little late, isn't it?
(HEAVILY ACCENTED) Dr. Gopnik, I believe the results
```

Examples from "Drunk Speech but Sober Captions" http://seanzdenek.com/

Provide alternatives to time-based media

In addition to captions, but never as a substitute, it can also be useful to provide a completely separate alternative for time-based media, such as a transcript or a text version of the information with appropriate images. These alternatives are useful in many situations:

- Users may have a device without audio output or don't want to use audio for some reason of their own.
- People who do not speak the language well may find it easier to understand the information in written form.
- People who need more time to review and understand verbal information benefit from being able to work at their own pace.
- A transcript can be printed.
- Search engines can read the transcript, but not the audio file.

For a usable, equitable experience, be sure the link to the transcript is easy to find near the media controls. Figure 9.9 shows one way to combine a video of the presenter, a clear view of the slides, and a synchronized transcript of the text. Users can adjust the size of each window.

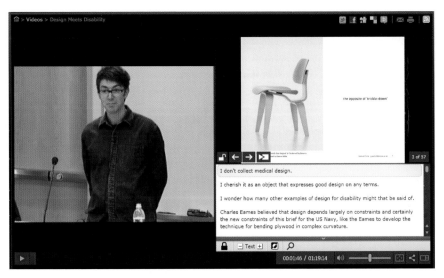

FIGURE 9.9

Screen shot of a talk by Graham Pullin, author of *Design Meets Disability*.
(http://research.microsoft.com/apps/video/default.aspx?id=103405)

Use dynamic elements carefully

Anyone who spends time on the web will at some point encounter a
website that overwhelms the senses, with myriad moving, blinking, and
flashing elements all demanding attention. The experience is unpleasant
at best. Distractions can seriously impede comprehension and effective
use by getting in the way of focus. Some types of animation can trigger
physical reactions, such as seizures and migraines.

Don't design with blinking or flashing elements, including tight patterns
that "animate" organically, with closely spaced lines or dots that visually
vibrate. No one wants to create a design that might make someone ill!

In addition, don't include dynamic elements that engage without user
request, such as a video that plays automatically when the page loads, a
page that refreshes automatically, or a slideshow that advances automatically. These involuntary actions can be disruptive for all users
and lead to all sorts of coping behaviors—for example, narrowing the
browser window to hide ads in the right column, browsing with audio
muted to avoid embarrassing audio outbursts, or waiting through a
slideshow cycle to finish reading an entry of interest. We have all learned
how to "tune out" design elements that we think are irrelevant in order
to cope with distraction—sometimes to our detriment, when elements
that appear irrelevant are precisely what we are seeking.

Sign Language Interpretation

To reach the widest audience, consider providing sign language interpretation. This is an advanced option—in WCAG, it's a Level AAA checkpoint—but one worth considering for official information or if you want to reach a deaf audience.

Sign language is important for a good user experience because some people read sign language more easily than text. This is because sign language is a distinct language, with its own grammar, word order, and ways of signaling functions like asking a question. Most sign languages include gestures and facial expression as part of the language, used to add meaning. Sign language isn't just a word-for-word translation of spoken language.

Watch out for localization issues, too. Sign language is different from country to country. There are regional accents and dialects, just as there are in spoken language. Native sign language speakers are effectively bilingual, as most understand both the local sign language and written or spoken language.

FIGURE 9.10
Election debates in Taiwan provide sign language interpretation along with captions. (www. openideo.com/open/ voting/inspiration/ accessible-information)

Sign interpretation is usually done by a live interpreter, such as the person shown in the inset in Figure 9.10, but an interesting new option is sign language animations. Instead of using a live interpreter, researchers are working to develop systems that can use an animated avatar to sign. None of these projects is quite ready for prime time—they are certainly not as good as a live interpreter—but they could be a good alternative way to generate sign language from a caption or transcript file. This technique is already widely used in educational publishing, such as the World Federation of the Deaf 2007 video with animated sign language at www.youtube.com/watch?v=wW2KBXrPEdM.

A few research projects to watch (and you can find many more with a quick search):

- Virtual Humans Group, University of East Anglia
  www.uea.ac.uk/cmp/research/graphicsvisionspeech/vh
- DePaul University ASL Project
  http://asl.cs.depaul.edu/

Unrequested changes of context can be particularly disruptive for screen reader users, who don't always know when a change of context occurs on a page, like a slideshow update or a page refresh. Media files that auto-play can be particularly challenging, as the audio from the media interferes with screen reader output, making it difficult to find the control to stop playback.

Try to reduce distractions overall and play moving or audible elements only on user request. (See Chapter 5, "Easy Interaction," *Let users control the operation of the interface*, for more on reducing distractions.)

Make presentations accessible

You might not think of presentations as part of web design, but with so many presentations posted online at sites like Slideshare and Vimeo, they are also part of the web, so it's worth considering how accessible they are. The work to make your presentation accessible also helps people read the slides, even when they didn't see your talk (Figure 9.11).

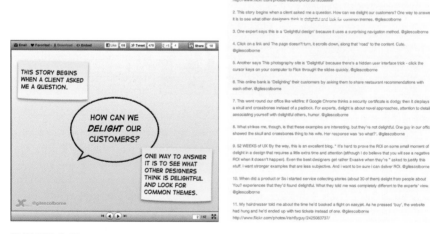

FIGURE 9.11

Giles Colborne uses a clever design to add a transcript to the presentations he posts on the site Slideshare: he adds a text box that looks like a Post-it note with a summary of his talk. Better yet, this takes advantage of the way Slideshare displays the text as a transcript at the bottom of the page. (www.slideshare.net/cxpartners/designing-for-delight-giles-colborne)

Some features to look for when you upload your slides:

- Can users download the presentation, in case they need to adjust the display to read the slides? Make the presentation itself accessible, too.
- Is the text of the slides displayed on the page, to provide an easily accessible version? If not, provide a link to the slide text.
- Is there a way to add a transcript of the verbal presentation?

You also need to make the presentation itself accessible. In Microsoft PowerPoint, you can add alt text to any images and check the reading order. You can also use the speaker notes to include longer descriptions of any charts, diagrams, or complex images.

Who Is Responsible for Accessible Media?

The most important work in creating accessible media—alternative text, captions, and transcripts—is the responsibility of the content team. It is up to the authors and producers to provide these text equivalents, to make the decisions about what is meaningful (or not) in supporting the overall content on the site, and to make it easy for users to find links to transcripts or other features that support accessible media.

The whole team also has a responsibility for choosing accessible media players or other widgets. This means choosing a player with buttons that work through the keyboard and where control icons have good alt text. Whether you are building the feature, using a widget from a library, or linking to a site like YouTube to embed video, if the player isn't accessible, your media won't be either. Make sure that the media players you choose have easy interaction and allow users to select closed captions, adjust the audio volume, and set display preferences.

WCAG 2.0 and Accessible Media

The guidelines for accessible media map to the following WCAG 2.0 requirements.

A site with plain language is **Perceivable**, providing alternatives to any media that relies on vision or hearing, including audio, video, animation, and presentations.

A site with accessible media meets the guidelines:

- **1.1 Text Alternatives:** Provide text alternatives for any non-text content (Guideline).
- **1.2 Time-based Media:** Provide alternatives for time-based media (Guideline).
- **2.3 Seizures:** Do not design content in a way that is known to cause seizures (Guideline).

The requirements for accessible media are:

- **1.1.1 Non-text Content:** All images or non-text content has a text alternative (Level AAA), except for images used for controls, CAPTCHA or other tests, or images used for decoration only (Level A).
- **1.3.3 Sensory Characteristics:** Instructions do not rely solely on sensory cues (Level A).
- **1.4.1 Use of Color:** Color is not the only way to communicate meaning (Level A).
- **1.4.2 Audio Control:** If any audio on a web page plays automatically for more than three seconds, the user can either stop it or adjust the volume without affecting the overall system volume level (Level A).
- **1.4.7 Low or No Background Audio:** Spoken word audio has no background noise, or allows the background sound to be turned off (Level AAA).
- **2.2.2 Pause, Stop, Hide:** The user can control moving, blinking, scrolling, or auto-updating information (Level A).
- **2.3.1 and 2.3.2 Flashes:** Web pages do not contain anything that flashes more than three times in any one-second period (Level AAA), or the flash is below the general flash and red flash thresholds (Level A).

Time-based media and caption requirements are:

- **1.2.1 Audio-only and Video-only (Prerecorded):** There are alternatives for pre-recorded audio-only and pre-recorded video-only media (Level A).
- **1.2.2 and 1.2.4 Captions:** Captions are provided for all audio content in synchronized media that is pre-recorded (Level A) or live (Level AA).

- **1.2.3 and 1.2.5 Audio Description or Media Alternative:** An alternative description of the video content is provided for synchronized media that is pre-recorded (Level A) or live (Level AA).

- **1.2.6 Sign Language (Pre-recorded):** Sign language interpretation is provided for all pre-recorded audio content in synchronized media (Level AAA).

- **1.2.7 Extended Audio Description (Pre-recorded):** When there is not enough time for audio descriptions in the video, extended audio description is provided for all prerecorded video content in synchronized media (Level AAA).

- **1.2.8 and 1.2.9 Media Alternative:** An alternative for time-based media is provided for all pre-recorded synchronized media and for all pre-recorded video-only media (Level AAA) and for live audio-only content (Level AAA).

The full text of the WCAG 2.0 requirements can be found in Appendix B.

Summary

Creating accessible media requires alternatives, so that the media content supports all the senses. It is the one type of content where a single version is not enough.

Types of alternatives include descriptions of images (called *alt text*), captions for video files, transcripts for audio files, and descriptions of any other non-text content that is not communicated in any other way.

To support different types of perception, color is used in combination with other cues for meaning, and instructions do not rely on visual cues.

Accessible media also includes presentation slides that are posted on the web.

Larry Goldberg is Director of the Carl and Ruth Shapiro Family National Center for Accessible Media (NCAM) at WGBH Boston, one of the most accessibility-aware media companies in the world. In addition to producing award-winning, captioned, and described television and web programs, WGBH hosts the National Center for Accessible Media, or NCAM, a research and development group focused on ensuring equity in media access. Larry oversees NCAM, where his dedication to developing technologies, policies, and practices to support accessible media has been instrumental in mainstreaming captions and video description and other innovative technologies.

We asked Larry what we could learn from the process of bringing captioning to television that will help us mainstream accessible media on the web.

Integrated technology as the tipping point.
Captioned television is everywhere—in bars, airports, gyms—but that wasn't always the case. There was a time when captions were delivered via set-top boxes, purchased by deaf and hard-of-hearing viewers. The tipping point came when the capability for displaying captions was built into standard television sets.

Getting there wasn't easy. The first step was to dispel the notion that captions were costly and benefitted only a small number of viewers. "You don't want to forget the primary purpose—that deaf people needed captions—but when it became obvious that captions helped comprehension and late-night television watching, and when the TV production community saw that they could integrate captioning into the production process without a lot of time and expense, they said, 'Fine, go ahead.'"

Most web media players can have caption display capacity built in; however, in most cases, captions are not required. In the United States, captioning recently became required under the new 21st Century Communications and Video Accessibility Act (CVAA), but only for previously broadcast video, not for user-generated or web-only video.

Becoming part of the process.
Process integration was key to mainstreaming captions. "We had to work fast so we didn't hold up delivery deadlines." This meant overnight shifts, better tools so captioners could work more quickly, and workflows that would integrate into production. "Once captioning became a line-item in budgets, and an expected check-point in the production flow, it became an accepted way of doing things."

Expectations for captioned television in bars and health clubs also helped. "When a TV producer goes to the gym every day and sees captions, and they look and go, 'Hey! There's an interview on—I want to know what he's saying!' Or they're at a bar and there's a game on, and they say, 'What just happened? Could somebody turn on the captions?' These wider circles of usage certainly help."

Enhancing media with accessible features.

With web-based digital technology, the broad benefits of accessibility features are even greater than with television. "In the earliest days, even in QuickTime 1.0, the benefits of searchability were fairly obvious," offering the ability to find key words in a video by searching a synchronized text track.

There is evidence that the presence of captions increases the attention to and time spent with video. "We believe captions are driving viewership and 'stickiness.'" And text has myriad benefits over other media when it comes to sharing. "If you have a text file of your media, it's much more readily shared. And you can tell people about it by pulling pieces of text out, posting or tweeting the text, and driving people to your media."

Making text from audio.

"It's the transcribing aspect that takes time." Most companies outsource because the expertise needed is not typically part of the media production team. Services like the WGBH Media Access Group make outsourcing easy, and prices have come way down. Plus, there's more to good captions than transcribing audio to text. "High-quality captions are crafted to make the captions more readable. Things like breaking the sentence in the right place, and removing captions during long pauses. Our captioners do everything in one step."

There are instances when outsourcing may not be necessary. A transcript or tele-prompter text can become the basis for captions. Services like YouTube's auto-timing work fairly well for synchronizing a prepared and accurate transcript with video.

Partnering with transcription software.

"You can't just take random, noisy, multi-speaker audio and expect high quality automatic transcription." But, with care, it's possible to transcribe a clean recording of clearly spoken audio using speech-to-text software like Dragon. "I know we want the tools to shape themselves to us and not us shape ourselves to the tools, but ... if you talk a little bit more robotically and enunciate properly, you can actually get a decent transcript using automatic speech recognition tools."

Adding captioning to the web media production workflow.

Integrating captions should be part of the post-production process of editing the media and digitizing for different platforms. "The people who know video and edit-ing tools get this."

profile continues on next page

Looking ahead for accessible media.

"With HTML5, you can link to different types of synchronized streams within the same web page." An instructional video containing information written on a board could display the same information in a new window as text. Or the information could be inserted into the video as a text track, and viewers can pause, listen to the synthesized text, and resume playing, making the content accessible to people who are blind or visually impaired.

Given the demonstrated value-added nature of captions and other accessibility features, Larry predicts that "as more captions come online as part of the new requirements, others not covered by the rules will too begin providing captions because they see the value."

CHAPTER 10

Universal Usability: Creates Delight

Amusement Park Rides

The Sensory Village at Morgan's Wonderland features a cluster of shops, each one offering activities to stimulate the senses. In the Auto Fix-It Shop, touch screens enable "designers" of all ages to create vehicles of their dreams and email the graphic representations to their home computers. (www.morganswonderland.com)

Theme park rides have come a long way from the physical thrills of roller coasters and Ferris wheels. The big theme parks have modern rides that combine a story with an environment to create an immersive experience appealing to all senses with motion, 3D movies, sound, touch, texture, and even smell. But there are also parks that let visitors create their own experience. Morgan's Wonderland in San Antonio, "the first-ever ultra-accessible family fun park," was designed as a place where everyone, regardless of their abilities, can have fun. Their attractions encourage imaginative play in a physically safe environment.

As technology and the web have changed from being a novelty to a part of daily life, expectations have also changed. More and more, it's possible to assume that technology will work, at least most of the time. That expectation is as true for people with disabilities as for anyone else.

In each of the chapters so far, we have shown how good design practice and accessibility go hand in hand. The same is true for usability. Once technical barriers are dealt with, you can focus on designing for usable accessibility, providing a good experience for everyone, and creating products that are not only usable, but even delightful to use.

How Universal Usability Supports Web Accessibility

Every time users have to struggle with operating a control, go into problem-solving mode to figure out where a link has taken them, or wonder what an image says, the website has taken them away from their own goal and broken the flow of the activity. Experiences such as these make products less usable and less enjoyable. They also make users feel less satisfied and successful.

With universal usability, **people can focus on the experience and their own goals because the product anticipates their needs.**

- **People can focus on their own activity or task.** When the technical barriers to accessibility are removed, it's possible to become immersed in the activity, rather than focusing on the mechanics of the interaction. The state of concentrated immersion is sometimes called *flow*. Mihaly Csikszentmihalyi, author of the book *Flow: The Psychology of Optimal Experience,* defines flow as a single-minded immersion in an activity or context. People experience flow when they are engaged in meeting a clear personal goal and have control over the activity. Direct and immediate feedback and intrinsic rewards of the challenge help them lose self-consciousness and become absorbed into the activity. Programmers, designers, and gamers talk about being "in the zone," when they are able to be highly productive and focused on their task. Flow happens when there is no friction between what you want to do and the software or website you are using to do it.

- **The site anticipates people's needs for information or interaction.** Instead of just plopping everything on the screen and letting users sort it out for themselves, delightful products are organized to provide what people need, when they need it, without overwhelming them with too much. A product that is helpful, informative, and useful can only be designed with a strong understanding of the audience.

Jacob

"Seeing color."

You might wonder why a blind person needs to know about colors. I can put labels in my clothes so I don't end up with clashing colors, but sometimes I need to know what color something is, like when someone tells me to get the "red folder." One of the coolest apps I've found recently lets me point my phone's camera at anything and then it reads the color name back to me. Is that a red pepper or a green pepper? It's a whole new kind of independence.

That's a practical use, but I learned about this app from an article that had this poetic description of walking around a garden hearing all the different colors described. He called it mind-blowing. I agree.

How to Design for Universal Usability

The guidelines in earlier chapters supported universal usability by making sure that elements in the design of websites and apps didn't create barriers, and that content and functionality were provided in a way that was accessible to different modes of use. Like lean design or "mobile first," universal usability requires an understanding of users and their goals to create sites that seem simple and transparently easy, even if the activity is complex.

Designing for universal usability builds on this foundation, pulling together the principles in this book to go beyond *technical* accessibility and basic requirements to create a good experience for everyone. The most innovative products not only lower the "costs" by removing frustrations, but also help people reach a sense of delight in a seamless interaction, raising the "benefits." The emotions produced in the relationship between cost and benefit are shown in Figure 10.1.

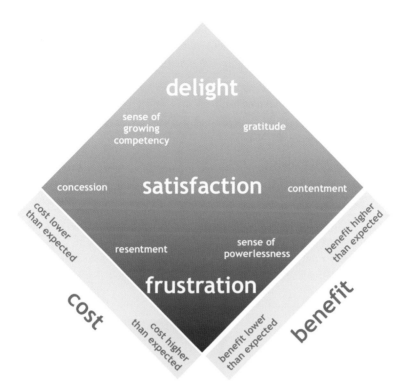

FIGURE 10.1

In B.J. Fogg's visualization, the Diamond of User Emotion, delight requires mastery, that is, a growing sense of competency and gratitude for a higher-than-expected benefit. (www.bjfogg.com/innovation.html)

Design for exploration and discovery

Sometimes the fun is in finding your own way through a site, whether it's a site for information, play, or staying connected. The goal of designing for exploration and discovery is to encourage users to try something new or follow a tangent, feeling safe in doing so.

Design for direct manipulation

When Ben Shneiderman first coined the term *direct manipulation,* most software was controlled through commands, often typed into a text interface. He suggested that designs that made actions rapid, incremental, and reversible would reduce errors and encourage exploration. Many mobile apps (and web apps influenced by mobile design) now incorporate direct interaction with objects on the screen, showing the results of actions immediately.

A good example of successful direct manipulation is the spreading and pinching gestures used to zoom in and out on a mobile device or tablet. Contrast how immediate the feedback is compared with changing the size of the image by entering a percentage or even by dragging a separate slider control.

In early direct manipulation interfaces, feedback was often presented only visually. It's important to include a way for the results of an action to be presented nonvisually as well, with a description or tactile feedback.

Apple's iPhone is an excellent example of a direct manipulation interface that is accessible, whether or not you can see the controls. The VoiceOver screen reader announces and describes elements in the interface and provides feedback about interactions with the interface (Figure 10.2).

FIGURE 10.2
VoiceOver uses both voice and gestures to interact with the iPhone. (www.apple.com/accessibility/iphone/vision.html)

Disclose the right things at the right time

Instead of dumping everything onto the screen at once, think about how much information or how many different features are needed at any point in an interaction. This technique, called "progressive disclosure," is commonly used in software interaction to manage complexity. For example, application menus typically contain the most commonly used features, with secondary features accessible via submenus.

Using progressive disclosure, or layering information, you can reveal the right amount of information at the right time, with the most important information first. There are many different ways to design for progressive disclosure.

- Show the most basic (or critical) information with a way to see more, for example, by using an accordion or a show/hide control. This can help make information easier to scan by making hidden content available with an easy (and easily reversible) action.

- Reveal additional features only when needed, such as when a controlling field is filled in, a condition is met, or when a user requests them.

What's important for accessibility is that the disclosed content comes *after* the trigger that discloses it so that assistive technology will find it in the proper place in the reading sequence (see Figure 10.3). ARIA should also be used to communicate content changes that occur as the result of using interactive elements. (See Chapter 5, "Easy Interaction," *Use WAI-ARIA for complex elements.*)

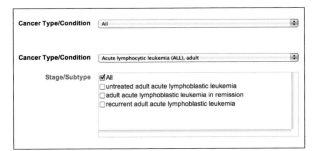

FIGURE 10.3
On the National Cancer Institute search page, the secondary selection is only revealed after first choosing the type of cancer.

Games Are a Window to the World

The AbleGamers Foundation (**www.ablegamers.com**) estimates that 33 million people with disabilities use online games. They see games as more than a way to fill time or an amusement.

Games may be a way to make friends or socialize when other communication or face-to-face meeting is difficult. As they put it, "For many people with disabilities, games offer a window to the world."

The group works to support gamers with disabilities and to help game developers create games that are more inclusive. Their companion website, Includification (**www.includification.com**), spells out guidelines for games accessibility by type of disability, with examples. A booklet puts the guidelines in a single 48-page resource for console and personal computer games.

Give rewards

Gamification is an interaction technique that aims to make common tasks more interesting by encouraging emotional engagement with the interface. One of the most basic techniques is the reward: points or badges that acknowledge steps in an activity or achievements toward a goal.

Think of rewards as a souped-up progress bar that adds status information and encouragement to the basic information associated with a task. You can also reward exploration by acknowledging discoveries, such as acknowledging a user for trying a new feature or finding new information.

Games and social applications also provide good signposting through status indicators. Levels (like the ones shown in Figure 10.4) are a cue not only for progress but also for the difficulty of a task (like ratings for ski slopes). Reputation points (and associated levels) act as a quick indicator for the rank of another user. Status indicators can help users stay oriented, especially when consistent indicators are presented in words and audio as well as visually.

FIGURE 10.4
In the Apple support forums, members gain points by answering questions and by how other members rate their answers. The levels are shown in both icons (with color and shape) and text.

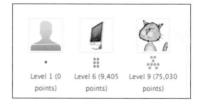

Support beginners and experts

In addition to thinking about how to make the web accessible to an audience with different abilities and using diverse technologies, for universal usability, Ben Shneiderman says we must also "bridge the gap between what users know and what they need to know." In some ways, this facet is the most difficult, as it requires an adaptable approach not only in design and technology but also in content and functionality. However, as Ben points out, the benefits are enormous. (See *Toward Universal Usability with Ben Shneiderman* in the profile in this chapter.)

In Chapter 8, "Plain Language," *Provide plain language summaries of complex content,* we described how the National Cancer Institute provides different types of health information, creating a bridge between patients and family and professionals. And it's a two-way bridge: in some cases professionals are novices, and vice versa—patients and family through necessity can sometimes become as knowledgeable as professionals about certain conditions.

In interface design, bridging the gap comes in many forms. One is with the help information, where instructions appear in the basic interface and are available only on request. Novice users may make extensive use of a supporting help feature until they grow proficient with the site. And since the more comprehensive help is easily available, it does not get in the way of expert users.

Another approach is to provide different methods for accomplishing the same task. Amazon's "1-Click" shopping supports frequent buyers who are confident in their selection, account setup, and in the services Amazon provides. New or infrequent Amazon shoppers will likely want to go the more traditional "shopping cart" route, which offers more opportunities to review and confirm purchasing details.

Create a conversation

Too often, sites talk *at* users. They push information at them based on an assumption about what they came to learn or do. The rise of social media and user-generated content can be a wake-up call to change that approach. When users contribute to a site, the conversational nature of good user experience becomes easy to see. But even sites without comments or other social features should have elements that engage users in conversation.

Layer information

As a metaphor for layering information, Leslie O'Flahavan and Marilynne Rudick from E-Write (**www.ewriteonline.com**) talk about creating bites, snacks, and meals, and serving up just the right amount at a time. In their definition:

- A bite is a headline with a message.
- A snack is a concise summary.
- A meal is the complete information.

News and shopping sites layer information naturally, allowing users to decide how much detail they want by presenting an article or product description as a heading and teaser paragraph, linked to the full detail page.

Twitter is an application built around the concept of layering. Think about a super-short tweet, with a link to a short blog entry, with a link to a longer article. The tweet is the bite, the blog entry is the snack, and the full article is the meal, and users get to choose, each step of the way, how much information they want to consume.

These layers can all be on one page, but more typically they are on separate pages connected by links. You can also use progressive disclosure to reveal hidden information as needed.

A layered approach to accessing information is particularly helpful for users who have a limited view of a web page, such as when using screen magnification software, which shows only a small portion of the screen at one time, or reading on the smaller screens of a mobile device. With good use of layering, users get enough information to make an informed decision about whether to take the next step toward learning more.

Tell a story

Stories persuade instead of commanding action. Telling a story can explain not just what a site does but also why it will be a valuable experience. Stories help users try new things or change their behavior because they allow them to imagine themselves in new situations. In effect, the story creates a conversation, asking users who they want to be, and then suggesting ways to reach that goal. A story can also offer motivation, either real or imaginary (like the zombies in Figure 10.5).

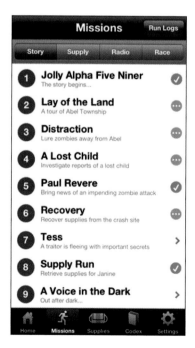

FIGURE 10.5

Most running apps track your stats, but Zombies, Run! mixes physical training with stories of "gripping missions" that involve outrunning a pack of zombies, as a way of motivating you to get out and run—fast! (www.zombiesrungame.com)

Be informative and helpful

Labels, prompts, instructions, and feedback in the interface serve the important role of helpful assistant—not one who bosses users around, or bores them with too much information, but one who seems to always be able to anticipate what's needed, and provides just the right guidance at the right time.

Provide an overview

Let users see the scope of a task or activity.

- Show all of the steps, so the scope is clear.
- Show relationships, such as the order in which steps must be completed.
- Show progress through the steps.

Keeping users oriented is especially important if a task is spread across more than one page, crosses devices, or has to be completed over time, such as setting up a bank account, shown in Figure 10.6.

Give instructions at the right time, in the right place

A big block of instructions at the top of the page is easily forgotten as a user works through a form or other interaction. Prompts or labels that display after a form field can come too late, after the field has been completed. Confirmation and error messages that display out of context are easily overlooked. Good help is not something users have to look for. It's there, where and when it's needed.

- Put preparation instructions or an overview at the beginning of the process.
- Put more detailed instructions just before they are needed.
- Offer extra help or tips for completion via a link to a help feature. Make sure the link displays before the action it supports, and that the feature is built to be accessible.
- Put interactive feedback, such as confirmation that an entry is formatted correctly or an alert that the information was not entered correctly, after the element in the linear sequence. (See Chapter 5, *Provide accessible instructions and feedback.*)

Your account name and number are shown as they will appear on the debit card.

After each step, a check mark appears to confirm that you completed it correctly.

Instructions not only tell you what to do but also why you are doing it.

You can see the whole page, but sections of the form only become active when you are ready to complete the step.

a

b

FIGURE 10.6

(a) Simple takes customers through the process of applying for an account through the company's partner bank, Bancorp. Once approved, the customer is seamlessly guided through creating a password and installing Simple's mobile application, an integral component of its online banking experience. (b) This view shows how the customer is guided through signing into Simple's web app for the first time.

Emily

Tell me what I need in advance.

When I go online, I just want to do things like everyone else. Most of the time, my disability doesn't slow me down, but when you mix having to get around in the real world with online forms, it can be a perfect storm of annoying barriers. Today, I'm trying to sign up for a seminar at my college. Why can't they tell me all the documents I'll need before I start this process? I got the form filled out, but when I went into the office this morning, I discovered that I needed to bring other documents with me. The online form didn't say anything about it. The whole trip was a big waste.

Practice usability for accessibility

Good design and accessibility guidelines are a good place to start, but to create something that delights your users, you have to get out and meet them. For universal usability, user research and usability testing are key activities at the beginning of the project and through all phases of design and development, not just at the end.

Do usability testing

If you aren't already testing your work, this is a good time to start. The days when usability only happened in expensive labs with an academic-style methodology are gone. In their place, we have rapid evaluation cycles that fit into an agile development process, testing with a small number of people at a time, using all sorts of remote and self-moderated testing tools.

Usability testing includes moderated sessions, in which you work directly with users:

- In their own environment (also called *field studies*)
- In a lab or conference room
- Over the web, using screen sharing and a voice connection

Usability testing also includes a wide range of self-moderated testing, in which you ask users to complete a set of activities using a tool that records what they do and their feedback. There are also tools that blend analytics with records of user activities, providing a view of how users navigate through your site.

One of the challenges for universal usability is the difficulty in matching accessibility guidelines to "common" assistive technology. Gregg Vanderheiden, the accessibility and universal design pioneer whose innovations are built into the Windows and Mac OS accessibility features, realized that standards are caught between two untenable options. Standards can either create guidelines that:

- Result in web pages that could be accessed using only the latest versions of the best (and most expensive) assistive technologies.

- Work with most AT but would severely limit web content to just basic web technologies.

Raising the Floor (raisingthefloor.org) is dedicated to solving this problem. It's an international collaboration of developers, advocates, researchers, and web designers with a mission: To make web and mobile technologies accessible to everyone with disability, literacy, and age-related barriers, regardless of their economic status.

The goal of the project is to create a *Global Public Inclusive Infrastructure* (gpii.net and gpii.net/Cloud4All) that can make access technology available on any website or connected device, raising the base level of accessibility for everyone, no matter where they are. They call it anytime, anywhere, any computer access, using automatic personalization of the user interface, based on user preferences stored in the cloud.

Each information and communication technology (ICT) device will be able to instantly change to fit users as they encounter the device, rather than requiring users to figure out how to adapt, configure, or install access features they need.

Usability testing reveals opportunities to improve the user experience. Take what you learn from observing behaviors and collecting feedback to refine your approach and improve your designs. Then you can correct issues that trip up your users and streamline tasks so that users are more successful with your product and have more fun using it.

Include people with disabilities in usability work

It's hard to create a good experience relying only on compliance with principles, standards, and regulations. That's especially true for universal usability. The accessibility standards, like WCAG 2.0, are written not only to solve a problem, but also to make it easy to test a site and know if it meets the standard. They get you part of the way, but not all the way to universal usability. If you don't include usability testing with people who use assistive technologies, you will never know whether you have created a site that goes beyond accessibility to create delight for people with disabilities.

For more about the importance of usability for accessibility, see Chapter 2, "People First," "Know Your Audience." For information about and resources for integrating usability testing into the design process, see Chapter 11, "In Practice." In particular, check out the usability information and tools listed in Appendix C, "More Reading."

Who Is Responsible for Universal Usability?

The entire team plays a key role in building in the features that make for a delightful user experience. Strategies and techniques for good interface design and universal usability must be part of the designs.

User research and usability are key activities for universal usability. User research is typically part of defining the purpose and design at the start of a project. Ideally, usability testing is integrated into each step of the process, allowing the team to prototype, test, and refine concepts before moving to the next phase in the design and development process. Usability testing is also part of the QA phase, to ensure that the finished product can be used successfully.

Summary

Although it's important to meet basic guidelines for accessibility, our goal is much more inclusive: to create a good user experience for everyone, including people with disabilities.

Universal usability helps technology "disappear" so that people can focus on their own activities. It relies on user research and usability testing to create designs that can anticipate users, acting as an assistant rather than directing the interaction.

Designing for universal usability allows people to explore safely and interact in a direct way. It layers information and activities so that users are not overwhelmed, and it acknowledges their achievements, and lets them control the flow of the activity, as well as the interface itself.

For over 30 years, Human-Computer Interaction (HCI) pioneer Ben Shneiderman has worked to keep the "human" in HCI broadly defined. Through research and teaching, writing and speaking, convening and facilitating, he has advocated for and assisted in the creation of technology tools in support of the common good. His award-winning book, Leonardo's Laptop: Human Needs and the New Computing Technologies, *is a call to action, urging users to expect success from their technology tools, and challenging designers and developers to satisfy those expectations.*

Since Ben invented the concept of universal usability, we wanted to get his take on how designers are measuring up, and what is keeping them from moving forward more effectively.

We are making progress toward universal usability.

In his May 2000 *Communications of the ACM* article, Ben raised the bar from accessibility to "universal usability," going beyond technical accessibility for people with disabilities to successful use of computers by everyone.[1] Now, more than a decade later, Ben is optimistic, citing examples including mobile apps, mobile phones, and digital cameras where "most people can succeed most of the time."

To illustrate, Ben tells a story of a recent plane trip. He was seated next to a businesswoman who was blind, which he knew because of the cane he helped tuck away in the overhead bin. "She sat down next to me, took out her iPad and keyboard, plugged in her earphones, and began to work." During the flight, Ben had the opportunity to chat with her. "I asked whether she was using special software and she said no." The current implementation on the Apple iPad provided everything she needed to do her work. "That's the kind of progress that inspires me in a wonderful way. It is gratifying to know that thoughtful design enables users with disabilities to hold challenging jobs and lead more fulfilling lives."

Universal usability is about satisfying experiences.

"'Accessibility' defines a set of technical requirements that could be met and yet the result may not be universally usable. 'Universal usability' specifies not just the attributes of the technology but the experience of the users." Universal usability is measured by way of real users, which, Ben acknowledges, "is a serious challenge."

"The expectation of satisfying the full range of human diversity is an enormously high achievement to push toward." But he also believes it is achievable, if everyone

---

1 http://www.cs.umd.edu/~ben/p84-shneiderman-May2000CACMf.pdf

makes it a priority. "Health is achievable. We have times when our health is better than others, but we strive to be healthy all the time." Similarly, we should strive to satisfy people "with different hardware, different network connections, different abilities, and different levels of knowledge about using computer technology."

Expecting to be successful in our use of technology.
Much has to do with our expectations as consumers of technology—whether we expect to be satisfied, or to satisfice.

Take, for example, digital cameras. We started out with small digital cameras that were able to take fuzzy images, and "we now expect to be able to take good photos indoors without a flash on a cell phone."

But, in many cases, our expectations have not been forceful enough to affect change. Software still produces "frustration and difficulty." University and commercial websites are not accessible. Even government agency websites that are under strict legal requirements to be accessible often aren't. To make real gains, every user must become an activist, speaking up to influence those who can make change happen.

Strategies for delivering universally usable experiences.
One approach to designing universally usable software is using multi-layer interfaces. Ben calls these "karate interfaces," in that users move metaphorically from white belt to black, mastering different skills at each step to build proficiency. "More attention to multi-layer interfaces could make systems usable by people with low skills and low needs, as well as people with high ability and high needs."

Ben recognizes that this type of interface requires more effort to build, but asserts, "It's something we should all expect. Moderate effort by the design team can bring huge benefits for millions of users."

> We expect automobiles to have levels of adjustability. We can move the seat, tilt the steering wheel, angle the mirrors, raise the lighting. Of course, it takes more time to design and may cost more, but the benefits to usability and safety are enormous.
>
> Mature technologies have many forms of adjustability that are easy to use, enabling people to move gracefully from simple use to more elaborate use. They empower people to do remarkable things.

profile continues on next page

Building awareness and expertise in the profession.

The main force holding accessibility back is lack of knowledge in the profession. Ben suggests a universal usability review for textbooks. "That kind of review would make authors, adopters, professors, and university departments aware that universal usability is an essential part of computer science." Ideally, the topic would be integrated into every aspect of the book, as with Ben's seminal textbook, *Designing the User Interface: Strategies for Effective Human-Computer Interaction*, with Catherine Plaisant, Maxine Cohen, and Steven Jacobs. In the current 5th edition, Ben notes that "There is no chapter about universal usability—the whole book is about universal usability!"

There is a growing movement in support of software engineer certification. I'm in favor of that, and I think one of the criteria should be that their training covers accessibility and universal usability. Universal usability shouldn't be a special course that someone has to take. It should be part of the preparation for anyone who learns about computer science and training for every computing professional. I want to be in a discipline and part of a profession that is proud of its role in achieving universal usability.

CHAPTER 11

In Practice:
An Integrated
Process

CHAPTER 12

The Future: Design for All

So far, we have focused on the process of designing. We've peeled back the layers of websites or web applications, and examined different principles, guidelines, and best practices that go into making a web for everyone. We have shown that by including a wider range of people and devices in your thinking, accessibility becomes an extension of good design, and people with diverse abilities and contexts can use the web successfully and enjoyably (see Table 12.1).

In the future, **everyone is part of making a web for everyone.**

TABLE 12.1 A WEB FOR EVERYONE

Principle	What It Does	Why It Is Important
People First	Designing for differences	People are the first consideration, and sites are designed with the needs of everyone in the audience in mind.
Clear Purpose	Well-defined goals	People enjoy products that are designed for the audience and guided by a defined purpose and goals.
Solid Structure	Built to standards	People feel confident using the design because it is stable, robust, and secure.
Easy Interaction	Everything works	People can use the product across all modes of interaction and operating with a broad range of devices.
Helpful Wayfinding	Guides users	People can navigate a site, feature, or page following self-explanatory signposts.
Clean Presentation	Supports meaning	People can perceive and understand elements in the design.
Plain Language	Creates a conversation	People can read, understand, and use the information.
Accessible Media	Supports all senses	People can understand and use information contained in media, such as images, audio, video, animation, and presentations.
Universal Usability	Creates delight	People can focus on the experience and their own goals because the product anticipates their needs.

To end the book, we'd like to take a step back and look at what it means to have a web that is designed and built for everyone, and identify what it will take to get there.

Web accessibility is all of our responsibility. It cannot be realized unless we all make a commitment and work toward a shared vision for the future. Other voices join ours in this look into the future, weighing in, sharing perspectives on what a web for everyone is and what we need to get there. In the end, we ask you to add your voice.

What a Web for Everyone Looks Like

As we worked on this book, we engaged in conversations at conferences, on lists, and on social media. We asked people what they thought it would mean to have a web for everyone, and how we would know when we had achieved it. Four big themes emerged.

- **It will be flexible.** We will all have the option to choose how we interact with the web. People have very specific needs and favorite emerging technologies, from voice control to specialized visual presentation. A web for everyone will let everyone interact in the way they like best.

  > People will be able to use affordable technology to consume, view, hear, or feel the information in the way that suits them best.
  >
  > —Alan Dalton, Accessibility Development Advisor
  > National Disability Authority (Ireland)

- **It will be ubiquitous.** Accessibility will be built into every site from the ground up. The operating systems and browsers, and building blocks like programming toolkits and website templates, will all start accessible. The work to build accessibility support into everything, from basic languages like HTML5 and popular platforms like WordPress and jQuery, is the basis for this future.

  > Learning to code to standards, and then actually being required to do so, will be enough.
  >
  > —Jennifer Sutton, Independent Consultant

- **It will be central to our work process.** Dozens of people pointed out that all the "ilities"—reliability, quality, usability, security, and so on—must be part of the process from the beginning. None of them can be a single task, added at the end of a project, like one more feature; their principles must be "baked in." The same goes for accessibility.

> As we say, if it isn't usable for everyone, it can't be accessible to anyone. (Perhaps not strictly true, but it makes an important point.)
>
> —Cliff Tyllick
> Senior Manager, Web Accessibility

- **It will be invisible.** Like good design, good accessibility is invisible. It doesn't draw attention or require special consideration. It just works and makes people more successful.

> A web for everyone is a reflection of a universal acknowledgement that we are all human beings. We will know that we have reached it when we are no longer talking about it.
>
> —Christopher Phillips
> Web Developer and Disability Services Manager

What We Need to Do to Get There

William Gibson famously said, "The future is already here; it's just not evenly distributed." This is as true with accessibility as with anything else. It's easy to pay attention to cool new technologies, but much harder to focus on the basics like designing to standards and making a site or app accessible.

Get out in front with web accessibility

The future is already here. There are technology innovations that empower people with disabilities. Thinking back on our personas, we can see innovations that helped each of them use the web more easily.

- In 2010, when Apple introduced the first iPad, it included VoiceOver, giving Jacob a screen reader built into the operating system. Assistive Touch helps Emily interact more easily, and Guided Access gives Trevor the focused experience he needs.

- Voice recognition has gone from clunky to sleek with Siri in iOS and Voice Input in Android for Lea, Jacob, and Carol.

- YouTube supports captions for Steven, including multiple languages for Vishnu and Maria. For everyone, there are tools that make captions much easier to create.

In the few years we worked on this book, the pace of innovation has only increased. Look at your own technology, and you can probably find something that didn't exist (or work well enough to be common) just a few years ago, but that has changed your life in some way.

But the future is also unevenly distributed. Websites and web applications have not enjoyed the same careful attention to the needs of people with disabilities.

> Unfortunately, at present we tend to go two steps forward and one back, as new technologies come out.
>
> —David Andrews, Chief Technology Officer
> Minnesota State Services for the Blind

Some large companies embrace accessibility, on financial, medical, shopping, and entertainment sites. But there are still too many valuable, interesting sites and apps launched that are simply not accessible. It's unlikely that anyone on those teams consciously intended to exclude people with disabilities, but working with a disregard for accessibility has the same result.

> The pace of technological change, especially disruptive technologies, means that we are not heading toward a particular planned goal, but we are constantly playing catch-up with wherever technology takes us. Somehow, we need to make accessibility sexy and cool.
>
> — Steve Green, Test Partners, Ltd.

To start, we must put attention and resources toward web accessibility.

Build awareness and understanding of more diverse people

User experience—and a web for everyone—starts with people. After all, if you don't know your audience, how can you design for them?

The personas in this book are a first step. Perhaps they helped you think more widely about accessibility. As an early reviewer of the book said, "I had no idea that someone with fibromyalgia might have any special computer needs."

In a presentation about cross-cultural design, Jean-Luc Doumont said, "To sharpen your cross-cultural skills, experience more cultures first-hand." The same principle applies to accessibility: to sharpen your accessibility skills, get to know more people with disabilities.

It's not hard, if you take the time to look. After the Society for Technical Communication (STC) started writing accessibility guides to their conference, they discovered more benefits than they originally imagined. Wheelchair users said that they had the confidence to attend because of the information the guides provided.

> When you recruit people for usability testing or user research, make the point of welcoming people with disabilities—and then really do it. You might be surprised at the range of people you find and what they need to be successful.
>
> —Caroline Jarrett, User Experience Consultant

Get support for accessibility into mainstream products

Mainstream accessibility features in technology tools started when both Apple and Microsoft built access tools into the operating systems with tools like high contrast settings and StickyKeys, which let people type key combinations (like Ctrl+C) as a sequence, to minimize the physical effort and dexterity needed to operate a keyboard.

In the past, many sites offered built-in controls to allow users to enlarge text or change colors. But now, browsers can do much of the work with text settings and zoom. Apple also led the way to more flexible devices when it included VoiceOver in iPhones, iPads, and iPods.

> We will know when we have reached the goal when accessibility is not a separate consideration, when it is baked into the infrastructure and we don't have to worry about it.
>
> —David Andrews, Chief Technology Officer
> Minnesota State Services for the Blind

This trend is important because it's difficult for separate assistive technology products to keep up with innovations and new products, and it's difficult for their users to manage updates and changes. Jacob may enjoy the challenge of learning how to make new products work for him, but many people do not.

Many people complained that new versions of browsers and websites disabled adaptations that worked for them. Others dream of a time when their favorite technology will work better. Tema Frank who, like Lea, finds that just using a keyboard or mouse can be painful, dreamed of speech recognition so good that people could "interact with their computers *a la* Star Trek."

When features like Apple's Siri or the speech input on Android are part of everyone's mobile device, technologies can quickly go from an experimental novelty to a dream come true, with effective tools that people can count on.

> We'll know when we've reached this goal when, for example, how a screen reader works will no longer be relevant.
>
> — Jennifer Sutton, Independent Consultant

There are many more examples. Bar codes and QR codes have revolutionized commerce systems. They are used to inventory products as they arrive in the store, identify those products as they are bought, and route packages to customers. Those same QR codes can help consumers shop, providing links to detailed product information or pricing. And, they help people with visual disabilities identify packages. Personal code readers used to be big, clunky things, but now they are just another app on a smart phone.

> My goal is to make at least the software side of accessibility so that it is a utility. So it doesn't cost a user several hundred or several thousand dollars in some cases to acquire the AT that they need in order to be a productive person in their day-to-day life, in their work life, in their education, but rather it becomes something that businesses distribute, through their interfaces, software, environments.
>
> —Mike Paciello, The Paciello Group

Make accessibility part of how we think

Accessibility starts from the way we think about our work, from first inspirations to well beyond launch. Another common theme for the future was the need to incorporate accessibility thinking into education and training, in design, computer science, engineering, psychology, communications, and business.

For example, at Michigan State University, first-year engineering students are given projects that concern addressing the needs of people with disabilities. Sarah Swierenga, the Director of the Usability and Accessibility Research Center, points out what a profound influence this early exposure can have. "Once you've had to think deeply about disabilities and human diversity, you will always think about it. Accessibility will always be part of your work."

> Ten years ago, most people thought of websites as pages on a desktop computer, designed for people with perfect vision, perfect hearing, perfect motor skills, perfect memory, and perfect understanding. Now, designers, developers, owners, and users are regularly experiencing websites on multiple devices, at multiple sizes, in all sorts of conditions, and this will help them to empathize with users of all abilities.
>
> —Alan Dalton, Accessibility Development Advisor
> National Disability Authority (Ireland)

Don't launch until it's accessible

In Chapter 4, "Solid Structure," we looked at how web standards are an important step to accessibility and a web for everyone. Designing and building to standards is the solid base on which the site or app can be built. The next step is meeting the requirements in WCAG 2.0 and national regulations.

Web standards are like curb cuts. They have value beyond their original purpose. Curb cuts were originally created for people who used wheelchairs, but helped people with carts, strollers, bicycles, and luggage. Similarly, both responsive design and accessibility rely on strong standards for the broad benefits they create.

The commitment to accessibility can't stop there, however. Don't consider a site or app done until everyone can use it. It is unfortunate when a small, basic accessibility bug keeps some people from using a site, particularly when the problem could easily be prevented.

Make sure that the content is accessible with good headings (using correct markup), alt text for images, captions for video, and transcripts for audio. Steven, Jacob, Maria, Vishnu, and Trevor will all thank you, along with anyone who would rather skim through a text version of a speech or watch a video with the sound off.

Sometimes, the secret is to "just ask." When Gerry Gaffney interviewed Shawn Henry for his podcast, UXPod, she asked him to post it only when he had a transcript available so that both the recorded interview and the transcript would launch together. Now, that process is part of his normal routine.

Now, to the Future

And so we come to the end of this book, but not the end of the story. Your journey continues from here. It's up to you to make the good stories that take the vision of a web for everyone from theory to reality.

> We want to tell the good stories about those who have done the right thing and have done a good job. That will encourage others to follow.
>
> —Ben Shneiderman, Human-Computer Interaction Lab

Now, it's all up to you. See you—see everyone!—on the web.

Accessible UX Principles and Guidelines

TABLE A.1 ACCESSIBLE UX PRINCIPLES AND GUIDELINES

Accessible UX Principle	Guidelines
People First	**Designing for differences:**
	People are the first consideration, and sites are designed with the needs of everyone in the audience in mind.
	Know your audience.
Clear Purpose	**Well-defined goals:**
	People enjoy products that are designed for the audience and guided by a defined purpose and goals.
	Start with purpose and goals.
	Design for clarity and simplicity.
	Think "accessibility first."
	Make templates accessible.
	Choose an accessibility strategy.
Solid Structure	**Built to standards:**
	People feel confident using the design because it is stable, robust, and secure.
	Code content to be machine-readable.
	Code to standards.
	Use standard web technologies.
	Organize code for clarity and flow.
	Use stylesheets to separate content and presentation.
	Use semantic markup for content.
Easy Interaction	**Everything works:**
	People can use the product across all modes of interaction and operating with a broad range of devices.
	Identify and describe interactive elements.
	Use basic HTML codes correctly.
	Use WAI-ARIA for complex elements.
	Use features of the technology platform.
	Provide accessible instructions and feedback.
	Support keyboard interaction.
	Make controls large enough to operate easily.
	Let users control the operation of the interface.
	Design for contingencies.
	Allow users to request more time.

Accessible UX Principle	Guidelines
Helpful Wayfinding	**Guides users:** **People can navigate a site, feature, or page following self-explanatory signposts.** Create consistent cues for orientation and navigation. Present things that are the same in the same way. Differentiate things that are different. Provide orientation cues. Provide clear landmarks within the page. Provide alternative ways to navigate.
Clean Presentation	**Supports meaning:** **People can perceive and understand elements in the design.** Design simply. Minimize distracting clutter. Design for customization of the display. Support customization through the browser. Design content for easy comprehension. Use color contrast to separate foreground from background. Use visual and semantic white space. Provide enough space between lines of text. Use clean typography.
Plain Language	**Creates a conversation:** **People can read, understand, and use the information.** Write for your audience. Follow plain language guidelines for writing content. Support users through their tasks. Structure the whole page for scanning and understanding. Write sentences and paragraphs for easy scanning. Write helpful links. Use language your audience is familiar with, or provide definitions. Provide plain language summaries of complex content. Don't rely on readability formulas. Usability test your content.

Table continues on next page

Accessible UX Principle	Guidelines
Accessible Media	**Supports all senses:**
	People can understand and use information contained in media, such as images, audio, video, animation, and presentations.
	Don't use only color to communicate meaning.
	Provide instructions without relying on visual cues.
	Describe the content or meaning of images.
	Provide captions and descriptions for video.
	Format captions to enhance meaning.
	Provide alternatives to time-based media.
	Use dynamic elements carefully.
	Make presentations accessible.
Universal Usability	**Creates delight:**
	People can focus on the experience and their own goals because the product anticipates their needs.
	Design for exploration and discovery:
	• Design for direct manipulation.
	• Disclose the right things at the right time.
	• Give rewards.
	• Support beginners and experts.
	Create a conversation:
	• Layer information.
	• Tell a story.
	Be informative and helpful:
	• Provide an overview.
	• Give instructions at the right time, in the right place.
	Practice usability for accessibility:
	• Do usability testing.
	• Include people with disabilities in usability work.

Accessible UX Principle	Guidelines
In Practice	**An integrated process:**
	People and organizations consider accessibility integral to their work and products.
	Make accessibility the way you do business.
	Make a commitment to accessibility.
	Assess what's needed for an integrated practice:
	• Evaluate the current site.
	• Identify ways to allocate resources.
	• Identify opportunities to integrate accessibility into current processes.
	• Assess current knowledge and readiness.
	Support an integrated practice:
	• Set policies and develop training.
	• Choose content and development tools that support accessibility.
	• Create a style guide and media library.
	• Include people with disabilities.
	• Provide tools and assistive technology for ongoing evaluation.
	• Make accessibility part of site maintenance.

WCAG 2.0
Cross-Reference

The accessible UX principles and guidelines in this book are organized around the user experience and how the design and coding of a website supports users.

In this section, we have matched our accessible UX principles and guidelines with the guidelines and detailed requirements (called *success criteria*) in WCAG 2.0 so that you can see the technical requirements for accessibility that support accessible design. Where there is no corresponding WCAG requirement, we provide other helpful resources. Some WCAG 2.0 criteria match more than one accessible UX guideline, showing how different UX specialists share responsibility for creating a web for everyone.

For each accessible UX principle, we also identify which of the WCAG 2.0 principles that form the foundation of web accessibility (Perceivable, Operable, Understandable, and Robust) are important in thinking about creating an experience that includes everyone.

Your project may be aiming for one of the WCAG 2.0 levels of conformance (A, AA, and AAA). When you think about accessible UX, you may find that a higher level requirement is easy to meet for some guidelines, adding to the overall accessibility of your site.

TIP SUMMARY OF WCAG 2.0 GUIDELINES
AND SUCCESS CRITERIA

A quick reference table of WCAG 2.0 guidelines and success criteria and the chapters in the book where they are covered can be found at the end of this appendix. The list of Accessible UX principles and guidelines can be downloaded from the book site.

People First: Designing for Differences

People are the first consideration, and sites are designed with the needs of everyone in the audience in mind.

The personas in this book are examples of people with disabilities and how they use the web and technology. Designing for Inclusion (www.w3.org/WAI/users/Overview.html) has good materials on how people with disabilities use the web and how to involve users in web projects. Appendix C, "More Reading," has a list of resources on assistive technology and disability statistics.

Clear Purpose: Well-Defined Goals

People enjoy products that are designed for the audience and guided by a defined purpose and goals.

As a technical standard, WCAG 2.0 does not have much to say about strategy and goals; however, other documents of the Web Accessibility Initiative (WAI) do. In particular, Planning and Implementing Web Accessibility (www.w3.org/WAI/managing.html) has helpful guides for establishing support for accessibility. These materials provide useful background and context when thinking about the accessibility goals for a project.

Solid Structure: Built to Standards

People feel confident using the design because it is stable, robust, and secure.

The Accessible UX guidelines for solid structure map to the fourth principle of WCAG 2.0: **Robust.** That is, sites must be coded so that they can be read by a variety of browsers and other technologies for accessing the web, including assistive technologies. Solid structure is also important to make a site **Perceivable**.

TABLE B.1 SOLID STRUCTURE

Accessible UX	WCAG 2.0 (or other resources)
Code content to be machine-readable. Code to standards. Use standard web technologies. Use stylesheets to separate content and presentation. Use semantic markup for content.	**1.3.1 Info and Relationships:** Information, structure, and relationships conveyed through presentation can be programmatically determined, or are available in text (Level A). **3.1.1 Language of Page:** The default human language of each web page can be programmatically determined (Level A). **3.1.2 Language of Parts:** The human language of each passage or phrase in the content can be programmatically determined except for proper names, technical terms, words of indeterminate language, and words or phrases that have become part of the vernacular of the immediately surrounding text (Level AA). **4.1 Compatible:** Maximize compatibility with current and future user agents, including assistive technologies (Guideline). **4.1.1 Parsing:** In content implemented using markup languages, elements have complete start and end tags, elements are nested according to their specifications, elements do not contain duplicate attributes, and any IDs are unique, except where the specifications allow these features (Level A). **4.1.2 Name, Role, Value:** For all user interface components (including but not limited to: form elements, links and components generated by scripts), the name and role can be programmatically determined; states, properties, and values that can be set by the user can be programmatically set; and notification of changes to these items is available to user agents, including assistive technologies (Level A).
Organize code for clarity and flow.	**1.3.2 Meaningful Sequence:** When the sequence in which content is presented affects its meaning, a correct reading sequence can be programmatically determined (Level A). **2.4.3 Focus Order:** If a web page can be navigated sequentially and the navigation sequences affect meaning or operation, focusable components receive focus in an order that preserves meaning and operability (Level A).

Easy Interaction: Everything Works

People can use the product across all modes of interaction and operating with a broad range of devices.

The Accessible UX guidelines for easy interaction focus on the elements of the user interface, and map primarily to the WCAG 2.0 principle, **Operable.** Many of the WCAG 2.0 operability requirements are intended to ensure that users are able to interact with the site through assistive technology.

TABLE B.2 EASY INTERACTION

Accessible UX	WCAG 2.0 (or other resources)
Identify and describe interactive elements. Use basic HTML codes correctly.	**3.3.2 Labels or Instructions:** Labels or instructions are provided when content requires user input (Level A). **4.1.2 Name, Role, Value:** For all user interface components (including but not limited to: form elements, links and components generated by scripts), the name and role can be programmatically determined; states, properties, and values that can be set by the user can be programmatically set; and notification of changes to these items is available to user agents, including assistive technologies (Level A).
Use WAI-ARIA for complex elements.	WAI-ARIA (Accessible Rich Internet Applications) is a separate W3C standard for making dynamic content and controls accessible by adding codes that describe the widget or region of a page to assistive technology (**www.w3.org/WAI/intro/aria.php**). The WAI-ARIA Design Patterns provide instruction for creating accessible widgets (**www.w3.org/TR/wai-aria-practices/#aria_ex**).
Use features of the technology platform.	The WCAG 2.0 guidelines are written to be technology-neutral, covering both HTML and other programming languages, rather than writing prescriptive advice for how to implement the requirements of each system or platform. To provide implementation advice, each requirement is linked to information (called Sufficient Techniques and Advisory Techniques) about how to meet it. The full list of How to Meet WCAG 2.0 can be filtered by technology (**www.w3.org/WAI/WCAG20/quickref/**).

Table continues on next page

Accessible UX	WCAG 2.0 (or other resources)
Provide accessible instructions and feedback.	**1.3.2 Meaningful Sequence:** When the sequence in which content is presented affects its meaning, a correct reading sequence can be programmatically determined (Level A). **3.3.1 Error Identification:** If an input error is automatically detected, the item that is in error is identified and the error is described to the user in text (Level A). **3.3.2 Labels or Instructions:** Labels or instructions are provided when content requires user input (Level A).
Support keyboard interaction.	**2.1 Keyboard Accessible:** Make all functionality available from a keyboard (Guideline). **2.1.1 Keyboard:** All functionality of the content is operable through a keyboard interface without requiring specific timings for individual keystrokes, except where the underlying function requires input that depends on the path of the user's movement and not just the endpoints (Level A). **2.1.3 Keyboard (No Exception):** All functionality of the content is operable through a keyboard interface without requiring specific timings for individual keystrokes (Level AAA). **2.1.2 No Keyboard Trap:** If keyboard focus can be moved to a component of the page using a keyboard interface, then focus can be moved away from that component using only a keyboard interface, and, if it requires more than unmodified arrow or tab keys or other standard exit methods, the user is advised of the method for moving focus away (Level A). **2.4.3 Focus Order:** If a web page can be navigated sequentially and the navigation sequences affect meaning or operation, focusable components receive focus in an order that preserves meaning and operability (Level A). **2.4.7 Focus Visible:** Any keyboard operable user interface has a mode of operation where the keyboard focus indicator is visible (Level AA).
Make controls large enough to operate easily.	Because WCAG 2.0 emphasizes the ability to customize the interface, it does not include any requirements for the size and spacing of controls, especially for touch screens. However, guidelines for touch-screen voting systems provide some guidance, requiring a minimum size of 0.5 inches high and 0.7 inches wide, with at least 0.1 inches between touch controls in either direction.

Accessible UX	WCAG 2.0 (or other resources)
Let users control the operation of the interface.	**3.2 Predictable:** Make web pages appear and operate in predictable ways (Guideline).
	3.2.1 On Focus: When any component receives focus, it does not initiate a change of context (Level A).
	3.2.2 On Input: Changing the setting of any user interface component does not automatically cause a change of context unless the user has been advised of the behavior before using the component (Level A).
	3.2.5 Change on Request: Changes of context are initiated only by user request or a mechanism is available to turn off such changes (Level AAA).
Design for contingencies.	**3.3 Input Assistance:** Help users avoid and correct mistakes (Guideline).
	3.3.1 Error Identification: If an input error is automatically detected, the item that is in error is identified, and the error is described to the user in text (Level A).
	3.3.3 Error Suggestion: If an input error is automatically detected and suggestions for correction are known, then the suggestions are provided to the user, unless it would jeopardize the security or purpose of the content (Level AA).
	3.3.4 Error Prevention (Legal, Financial, Data): For web pages that cause legal commitments or financial transactions for the user to occur, that modify or delete user-controllable data in data storage systems, or that submit user test responses, at least one of the following is true (Level AA):
	3.3.5 Help: Context-sensitive help is available (Level AAA).
	3.3.6 Error Prevention (All): For web pages that require the user to submit information, at least one of the following is true (Level AAA):
	Reversible: Submissions are reversible.
	Checked: Data entered by the user is checked for input errors, and the user is provided an opportunity to correct them.
	Confirmed: A mechanism is available for reviewing, confirming, and correcting information before finalizing the submission.

Table continues on next page

Accessible UX	WCAG 2.0 (or other resources)
Allow users to request more time.	**2.2 Enough Time:** Provide users enough time to read and use content.
	2.2.1 Timing Adjustable: For each time limit that is set by the content, at least one of the following is true (Level A):
	Turn off: The user is allowed to turn off the time limit before encountering it; or
	Adjust: The user is allowed to adjust the time limit before encountering it over a wide range that is at least ten times the length of the default setting; or
	Extend: The user is warned before time expires and given at least 20 seconds to extend the time limit with a simple action (for example, "press the spacebar"), and the user is allowed to extend the time limit at least ten times; or
	Real-time Exception: The time limit is a required part of a real-time event (for example, an auction), and no alternative to the time limit is possible; or
	Essential Exception: The time limit is essential and extending it would invalidate the activity; or 20 Hour Exception: The time limit is longer than 20 hours.
	2.2.3 No Timing: Timing is not an essential part of the event or activity presented by the content, except for non-interactive synchronized media and real-time events (Level AAA).
	2.2.4 Interruptions: Interruptions can be postponed or suppressed by the user, except interruptions involving an emergency (Level AAA).
	2.2.5 Re-authenticating: When an authenticated session expires, the user can continue the activity without loss of data after re-authenticating (Level AAA).

Helpful Wayfinding: Guides Users

People can navigate a site, feature, or page following self-explanatory signposts.

The Accessible UX guidelines for helpful wayfinding map to the WCAG 2.0 principles, **Operable** and **Understandable**, with a focus on whether the operation of user interface is communicated clearly.

TABLE B.3 HELPFUL WAYFINDING

Accessible UX	WCAG 2.0 (or other resources)
Create consistent cues for orientation and navigation. Present things that are the same in the same way. Differentiate things that are different.	**2.4 Navigable:** Provide ways to help users navigate, find content, and determine where they are (Guideline). **2.4.4 Link Purpose (In Context):** The purpose of each link can be determined from the link text alone or from the link text together with its programmatically determined link context, except where the purpose of the link would be ambiguous to users in general (Level A). **2.4.9 Link Purpose (Link Only):** A mechanism is available to allow the purpose of each link to be identified from link text alone, except where the purpose of the link would be ambiguous to users in general (Level AAA). **3.2 Predictable:** Make web pages appear and operate in predictable ways (Guideline). **3.2.3 Consistent Navigation:** Navigational mechanisms that are repeated on multiple web pages within a set of web pages occur in the same relative order each time they are repeated, unless a change is initiated by the user (Level AA). **3.2.4 Consistent Identification:** Components that have the same functionality within a set of web pages are identified consistently (Level AA).
Provide orientation cues. Provide clear landmarks within the page.	**2.4.1 Bypass Blocks:** A mechanism is available to bypass blocks of content that are repeated on multiple web pages (Level A). **2.4.2 Page Titled:** Web pages have titles that describe topic or purpose (Level A). **2.4.6 Headings and Labels:** Headings and labels describe topic or purpose (Level AA). **2.4.8 Location:** Information about the user's location within a set of web pages is available (Level AAA). **2.4.10 Section Headings:** Section headings are used to organize the content (Level AAA). The WAI-ARIA specification provides guidance on how to use the ARIA landmark role to define page regions: see Providing Navigable Structure Within Web Pages (www.w3.org/TR/wai-aria-practices/#kbd_layout).
Provide alternative ways to navigate.	**2.4.5 Multiple Ways:** More than one way is available to locate a web page within a set of web pages, except where the web page is the result of, or a step in, a process (Level AA).

Clean Presentation: Supports Meaning

People can perceive and understand elements in the design.

The Accessible UX guidelines for clean presentation map to the WCAG 2.0 principle, **Perceivable**, ensuring that both content and interactive elements are presented to users in ways they can perceive.

TABLE B.4 CLEAN PRESENTATION

Accessible UX	WCAG 2.0 (or other resources)
Design simply. Minimize clutter.	As a technical standard, WCAG 2.0 has little to say about general design and usability principles.
Design for customization of the display. Support customization through the browser.	**1.3 Adaptable:** Create content that can be presented in different ways (for example, simpler layout) without losing information or structure (Guideline). **1.4.4 Resize text:** Except for captions and images of text, text can be resized without assistive technology up to 200 percent without loss of content or functionality (Level AA). **1.4.5 Images of Text:** If the technologies being used can achieve the visual presentation, text is used to convey information rather than images of text except for the following (Level AA): **Customizable:** The image of text can be visually customized to the user's requirements. **Essential:** A particular presentation of text is essential to the information being conveyed. **1.4.9 Images of Text (No Exception):** Images of text are only used for pure decoration or where a particular presentation of text is essential to the information being conveyed (Level AAA). **1.4.8 Visual Presentation:** For the visual presentation of blocks of text, a mechanism is available to achieve the following (Level AAA): **Foreground and background colors** can be selected by the user. **Text** can be resized without assistive technology up to 200 percent in a way that does not require the user to scroll horizontally to read a line of text on a full-screen window.
Design content for easy comprehension.	**2.4.6 Headings and Labels:** Headings and labels describe topic or purpose (Level AA). **2.4.10 Section Headings:** Section headings are used to organize the content (Level AAA). **3.3.2 Labels or Instructions:** Labels or instructions are provided when content requires user input (Level A).

Accessible UX	WCAG 2.0 (or other resources)
Use color contrast to separate foreground from background.	**1.4 Distinguishable:** Make it easier for users to see and hear content, including separating foreground from background. **1.4.3 Contrast (Minimum):** The visual presentation of text and images of text has a contrast ratio of at least 4.5:1, except for the following (Level AA): **Large Text:** Large-scale text and images of large-scale text have a contrast ratio of at least 3:1. **1.4.6 Contrast (Enhanced):** The visual presentation of text and images of text has a contrast ratio of at least 7:1, except for the following (Level AAA): **Large Text:** Large-scale text and images of large-scale text have a contrast ratio of at least 4.5:1. Both 1.4.3-Level AA and 1.4.6-Level AAA requirements include two other exceptions: **Incidental:** Text or images of text that are part of an inactive user interface component, that are pure decoration, that are not visible to anyone, or that are part of a picture that contains significant other visual content, have no contrast requirement. **Logotypes:** Text that is part of a logo or brand name has no minimum contrast requirement.
Use visual and semantic white space.	WCAG 2.0 does not provide guidance on how to best use visual white space to create groupings and describe the relationships among elements. It does address semantic white space in the following success criteria: **1.3.1 Info and Relationships:** Information, structure, and relationships conveyed through presentation can be programmatically determined or are available in text (Level A).
Provide enough space between lines of text. Use clean typography.	**1.4.8 Visual Presentation:** For the visual presentation of blocks of text, a mechanism is available to achieve the following (Level AAA): **Width** is no more than 80 characters or glyphs (40 if CJK). **Text** is not justified (aligned to both the left and the right margins). **Line spacing** (leading) is at least a space-and-a-half within paragraphs, and paragraph spacing is at least 1.5 times larger than the line spacing.

Plain Language: Creates a Conversation

People can read, understand, and use the information.

The Accessible UX guidelines for plain language map to the WCAG 2.0 principle that information and the operation of user interface must be **Understandable**.

TABLE B.5 PLAIN LANGUAGE

Accessible UX	WCAG 2.0 (or other resources)
Write for your audience.	**3.1 Readable:** Make text content readable and understandable (Guideline).
Follow plain language guidelines for writing content. Write sentences and paragraphs for easy scanning.	The U.S. Federal Plain Language Guidelines are an excellent source of guidance on writing using plain language (**www.plainlanguage.gov**).
Support users through their tasks. Structure the whole page for scanning and understanding.	**2.4.6 Headings and Labels:** Headings and labels describe topic or purpose (Level AA). **2.4.10 Section Headings:** Section headings are used to organize the content (Level AAA). **3.3.2 Labels or Instructions:** Labels or instructions are provided when content requires user input (Level A). **3.3.5 Help:** Context-sensitive help is available (Level AAA).
Write helpful links.	**2.4.4 Link Purpose (In Context):** The purpose of each link can be determined from the link text alone or from the link text together with its programmatically determined link context, except where the purpose of the link would be ambiguous to users in general (Level A). **2.4.9 Link Purpose (Link Only):** A mechanism is available to allow the purpose of each link to be identified from link text alone, except where the purpose of the link would be ambiguous to users in general (Level AAA).

Accessible UX	WCAG 2.0 (or other resources)
Use language your audience is familiar with, or provide definitions.	**3.1.1 Language of Page:** The default human language of each web page can be programmatically determined (Level A).
	3.1.2 Language of Parts: The human language of each passage or phrase in the content can be programmatically determined except for proper names, technical terms, words of indeterminate language, and words or phrases that have become part of the vernacular of the immediately surrounding text (Level AA).
	3.1.3 Unusual Words: A mechanism is available for identifying specific definitions of words or phrases used in an unusual or restricted way, including idioms and jargon (Level AAA).
	3.1.4 Abbreviations: A mechanism for identifying the expanded form or meaning of abbreviations is available (Level AAA).
	3.1.6 Pronunciation: A mechanism is available for identifying specific pronunciation of words where meaning of the words, in context, is ambiguous without knowing the pronunciation (Level AAA).
Provide plain language summaries of complex content. Don't rely on readability formulas.	**3.1.5 Reading Level:** When text requires reading ability more advanced than the lower secondary education level after removal of proper names and titles, supplemental content, or a version that does not require reading ability more advanced than the lower secondary education level, is available (Level AAA).
Usability test your content.	The WAI document, *Involving Users in Evaluating Web Accessibility* (**www.w3.org/WAI/eval/users.html**), has links to resources to ensure that both accessibility and usability testing include people with disabilities.

Accessible Media: Supports All Senses

People can understand and use information contained in media, such as images, audio, video, animation, and presentations.

The Accessible UX accessible media guidelines map to the WCAG 2.0 principles **Perceivable**, in making the content accessible through different senses, and **Understandable**, in that all users can operate the media interface.

TABLE B.6 ACCESSIBLE MEDIA

Accessible UX	WCAG 2.0 (or other resources)
Don't use only color to communicate meaning.	**1.4.1 Use of Color:** Color is not used as the only visual means of conveying information, indicating an action, prompting a response, or distinguishing a visual element (Level A).
Provide instructions without relying on visual cues.	**1.3.3 Sensory Characteristics:** Instructions provided for understanding and operating content do not rely solely on sensory characteristics of components such as shape, size, visual location, orientation, or sound (Level A).
Describe the content or meaning of images.	**1.1 Text Alternatives:** Provide text alternatives for any non-text content so that it can be changed into other forms people need, such as large print, braille, speech, symbols, or simpler language (Guideline).
	1.1.1 Non-text Content: All non-text content that is presented to the user has a text alternative that serves the equivalent purpose, except for the situations listed below (Level A):
	Controls, Input: If non-text content is a control or accepts user input, then it has a name that describes its purpose. (Refer to Guideline 4.1 for additional requirements for controls and content that accepts user input.)
	Time-Based Media: If non-text content is time-based media, then text alternatives at least provide descriptive identification of the non-text content.
	Test: If non-text content is a test or exercise that would be invalid if presented in text, then text alternatives at least provide descriptive identification of the non-text content.
	Sensory: If non-text content is primarily intended to create a specific sensory experience, then text alternatives at least provide descriptive identification of the non-text content.
	CAPTCHA: If the purpose of non-text content is to confirm that content is being accessed by a person rather than a computer, then text alternatives that identify and describe the purpose of the non-text content are provided, and alternative forms of CAPTCHA using output modes for different types of sensory perception are provided to accommodate different disabilities.
	Decoration, Formatting, Invisible: If non-text content is pure decoration, is used only for visual formatting, or is not presented to users, then it is implemented in a way that it can be ignored by assistive technology.

Accessible UX	WCAG 2.0 (or other resources)
Provide captions and descriptions for video. Format captions to enhance meaning.	**1.2.2 Captions (Prerecorded):** Captions are provided for all prerecorded audio content in synchronized media, except when the media is a media alternative for text and is clearly labeled as such (Level A).
	1.2.3 Audio Description or Media Alternative (Prerecorded): An alternative for time-based media or audio description of the prerecorded video content is provided for synchronized media, except when the media is a media alternative for text and is clearly labeled as such (Level A).
	1.2.4 Captions (Live): Captions are provided for all live audio content in synchronized media (Level AA).
	1.2.5 Audio Description (Prerecorded): Audio description is provided for all prerecorded video content in synchronized media (Level AA).
	1.2.7 Extended Audio Description (Prerecorded): Where pauses in foreground audio are insufficient to allow audio descriptions to convey the sense of the video, extended audio description is provided for all prerecorded video content in synchronized media (Level AAA).
Provide alternatives to time-based media.	**1.2 Time-based Media:** Provide alternatives for time-based media (Guideline).
	1.2.1 Audio-only and Video-only (Prerecorded): For prerecorded audio-only and prerecorded video-only media, the following are true, except when the audio or video is a media alternative for text and is clearly labeled as such (Level A):
	Prerecorded Audio-only: An alternative for time-based media is provided that presents equivalent information for prerecorded audio-only content.
	Prerecorded Video-only: Either an alternative for time-based media or an audio track is provided that presents equivalent information for prerecorded video-only content.
	1.2.6 Sign Language (Prerecorded): Sign language interpretation is provided for all prerecorded audio content in synchronized media (Level AAA).
	1.2.8 Media Alternative (Prerecorded): An alternative for time-based media is provided for all prerecorded synchronized media and for all prerecorded video-only media (Level AAA).
	1.2.9 Audio-only (Live): An alternative for time-based media that presents equivalent information for live audio-only content is provided (Level AAA).

Table continues on next page

Accessible UX	WCAG 2.0 (or other resources)
Use dynamic elements carefully.	**1.4.2 Audio Control:** If any audio on a Web page plays automatically for more than three seconds, either a mechanism is available to pause or stop the audio, or a mechanism is available to control audio volume independently from the overall system volume level (Level A).
	1.4.7 Low or No Background Audio: For prerecorded audio-only content that (1) contains primarily speech in the foreground, (2) is not an audio CAPTCHA or audio logo, and (3) is not vocalization intended to be primarily musical expression such as singing or rapping, at least one of the following is true (Level AAA):
	No Background: The audio does not contain background sounds.
	Turn Off: The background sounds can be turned off.
	20 dB: The background sounds are at least 20 decibels lower than the foreground speech content, with the exception of occasional sounds that last for only one or two seconds.
	2.2.2 Pause, Stop, Hide: For moving, blinking, scrolling, or auto-updating information, all of the following are true (Level A):
	Moving, blinking, scrolling: For any moving, blinking or scrolling information that (1) starts automatically, (2) lasts more than five seconds, and (3) is presented in parallel with other content, there is a mechanism for the user to pause, stop, or hide it unless the movement, blinking, or scrolling is part of an activity where it is essential; and
	Auto-updating: For any auto-updating information that (1) starts automatically and (2) is presented in parallel with other content, there is a mechanism for the user to pause, stop, or hide it, or to control the frequency of the update unless the auto-updating is part of an activity where it is essential.
	2.3 Seizures: Do not design content in a way that is known to cause seizures (Guideline).
	2.3.1 Three Flashes or Below Threshold: Web pages do not contain anything that flashes more than three times in any one-second period, or the flash is below the general flash and red flash thresholds (Level A).
	2.3.2 Three Flashes: Web pages do not contain anything that flashes more than three times in any one-second period (Level AAA).

Accessible UX	WCAG 2.0 (or other resources)
Make presentations accessible.	Presentations are not covered in WCAG 2.0, but *How to Make Presentations Accessible to All* (www.w3.org/WAI/training/accessible.php) covers everything about presentations, from planning the event to delivering the presentation.

Universal Usability: Creates Delight

People can focus on the experience and their own goals because the product anticipates their needs.

Universal usability builds on all of the guidelines from other chapters that keep operating and understanding—*using* the site or application—from getting in the way of exploration, discovery, and successful task completion. In this way, the Accessible UX guidelines for universal usability map to *all* of the WCAG principles, and guidelines support universal usability by supporting clear purpose, solid structure, easy interaction, helpful wayfinding, clean presentation, plain language, and accessible media.

Summary: WCAG Requirements in Order

TABLE B.7 UNIVERSAL USABILITY

Number	Level	Short Title	Chapter
1.1		**Text Alternatives**	**9**
1.1.1	A	Non-text Content	9
1.2		**Time-based Media**	**9**
1.2.1	A	Audio-only and Video-only (Prerecorded)	9
1.2.2	A	Captions (Prerecorded)	9
1.2.3	A	Audio Description or Media Alternative (Prerecorded)	9
1.2.4	AA	Captions (Live)	9
1.2.5	AA	Audio Description (Prerecorded)	9
1.2.6	AAA	Sign Language (Prerecorded)	9
1.2.7	AAA	Extended Audio Description (Prerecorded)	9
1.2.8	AAA	Media Alternative (Prerecorded)	9
1.2.9	AAA	**Audio-only (Live)**	9
1.3		Adaptable	**7**
1.3.1	A	Info and Relationships	4, 7
1.3.2	A	Meaningful Sequence	4, 5
1.3.3	A	**Sensory Characteristics**	9
1.4		Distinguishable	**7**
1.4.1	A	Use of Color	9
1.4.2	A	Audio Control	9
1.4.3	AA	Contrast (Minimum)	7
1.4.4	AA	Resize Text	7
1.4.5	AA	Images of Text	7
1.4.6	AAA	Contrast (Enhanced)	7
1.4.7	AAA	Low or No Background Audio	9
1.4.8	AAA	Visual Presentation	7
1.4.9	AAA	Images of Text (No Exception)	7

Number	Level	Short Title	Chapter
2.1		**Keyboard Accessible**	**5**
2.1.1	A	Keyboard	5
2.1.2	A	No Keyboard Trap	5
2.1.3	AAA	Keyboard (No Exception)	5
2.2		**Enough Time**	**5**
2.2.1	A	Timing Adjustable	5
2.2.2	A	Pause, Stop, Hide	9
2.2.3	AAA	No Timing	5
2.2.4	AAA	Interruptions	5
2.2.5	AAA	Re-authenticating	5
2.3		**Seizures**	**9**
2.3.1	A	Three Flashes or Below Threshold	9
2.3.2	AAA	Three Flashes	9
2.4		**Navigable**	**6**
2.4.1	A	Bypass Blocks	6
2.4.2	A	Page Titled	6
2.4.3	A	Focus Order	4, 5
2.4.4	A	Link Purpose (In Context)	6, 8
2.4.5	AA	Multiple Ways	6
2.4.6	AA	Headings and Labels	6, 7, 8
2.4.7	AA	Focus Visible	5
2.4.8	AAA	Location	6
2.4.9	AAA	Link Purpose (Link Only)	6, 8
2.4.10	AAA	Section Headings	6, 7, 8
3.1		**Readable**	**8**
3.1.1	A	Language of Page	4, 8
3.1.2	AA	Language of Parts	4, 8
3.1.3	AAA	Unusual Words	8
3.1.4	AAA	Abbreviations	8
3.1.5	AAA	Reading Level	8
3.1.6	AAA	Pronunciation	8
3.2		**Predictable**	**5, 6**
3.2.1	A	On Focus	5
3.2.2	A	On Input	5
3.2.3	AA	Consistent Navigation	6
3.2.4	AA	Consistent Identification	6
3.2.5	AAA	Change on Request	5
3.3		**Input Assistance**	**5**
3.3.1	A	Error Identification	5
3.3.2	A	Labels or Instructions	5, 7, 8
3.3.3	AA	Error Suggestion	5
3.3.4	AA	Error Prevention (Legal, Financial, Data)	5
3.3.5	AAA	Help	5, 8
3.3.6	AAA	Error Prevention (All)	5
4.1		**Compatible**	**4**
4.1.1	A	Parsing	4
4.1.2	A	Name, Role, Value	4, 5

More Reading

Chapter 1: A Web for Everyone

Design Principles

- *Change by Design: How Design Thinking Transforms Organizations and Inspires Innovation,* Tim Brown
- Principles of Universal Design: http://rfld.me/16DZjTm
- Research-Based Web Design and Usability Guidelines: http://rfld.me/1dhr9V0
- *Universal Principles of Design,* William Lidwell, Kritina Holden, and Jill Butler
- *Web Style Guide,* Patrick Lynch and Sarah Horton: http://rfld.me/HozHPp

Books on Web Accessibility

- *Access by Design: A Guide to Universal Usability for Web Designers,* Sarah Horton: http://rfld.me/18ukbHh
- *The Accessibility Handbook,* Katie Cunningham
- *Building Accessible Web Sites,* Joe Clark
- *Constructing Accessible Web Sites,* Jim Thatcher, Paul Bohman, Michael Burks, Shawn Lawton Henry, Bob Regan, Sarah Swierenga, Mark D. Urban, and Cynthia D. Waddell
- *Just Ask: Integrating Accessibility Throughout Design,* Shawn Lawton Henry
- *Maximum Accessibility,* John M. Slatin and Sharon Rush
- *Universal Design for Web Applications,* Wendy Chisholm and Matt May
- *Universal Usability: Designing Computer Interfaces for Diverse Users,* Jonathan Lazar (editor)
- *Web Accessibility for People with Disabilities,* Mike Paciello
- *Web Accessibility: Web Standards and Regulatory Compliance*, Richard Rutter, Patrick H. Lauke, Cynthia Waddell, and Jim Thatcher

Chapter 2: People First

User Research and Personas

- *The Persona Lifecycle*, Tamara Adlin and John Pruitt
- *User and Task Analysis for Interface Design*, JoAnn Hackos and Janice C. Redish
- Character Creator, Dana Chisnell: http://rfld.me/1gV3kHI

Disability Demographics and User Research

- World Health Organization: http://rfld.me/1ioAXx5

- Disability Statistics, Cornell University: http://rfld.me/17TnOXR

- The ADA, 20 Years Later, Harris Interactive, for the Kessler Foundation and National Organization on Disability: http://rfld.me/1cmpMaw

About Assistive Technology

- AbleData—Your source for assistive technology information: http://rfld.me/1hmQnEc

- Types of Assistive Technology Products, Microsoft Accessibility: http://rfld.me/1bv4i6m

- The Future of Inclusive Design Online, Clayton Lewis: www.fcc.gov/events/accessibility-innovation-initiative-speaker-series-presents-clayton-lewis-future-inclusive-de

- Assistive Technology for Individuals with Cognitive Impairments, Idaho Assistive Technology Project: http://idahoat.org/Portals/0/Documents/cognitive_impair.pdf

Personas of People with Disabilities

- Designing with People—Ten portraits based on real people from the Helen Hamlyn Centre for Design's user network: http://rfld.me/Hm1wr7

- Personas from the EU's AEGIS Project, Open Accessibility Everywhere: http://rfld.me/19MPKjj

- Disabled Personas, JASIG: http://rfld.me/16E7jUt

Chapter 3: Clear Purpose

- *Mobile First,* Luke Wroblewski

- *Simple and Usable: Web, Mobile, and Interaction Design,* Giles Colborne

Chapter 4: Solid Structure

Web and Accessibility Standards

- WAI ARIA: http://rfld.me/Hr7sP7

- Web Content Accessibility Guidelines 2.0: http://rfld.me/1gVdw2Q

- HTML (and XHTML): http://rfld.me/1atZhus
- CSS: http://rfld.me/1aAR3CQ
- JavaScript (EMCAScript): http://rfld.me/Hr7AhJ

Code Validators
- W3C HTML Validator: http://rfld.me/Hr7Ih3
- W3C CSS Validator: http://rfld.me/1cmxnWA
- WAVE Web Accessibility Validation Tool: http://rfld.me/16gDffl

Chapter 5: Easy Interaction

- *Defensive Design for the Web: How to Improve Error Messages, Help, Forms, and Other Crisis Points*, Matthew Linderman and Jason Fried
- *Forms that Work: Designing Web Forms for Usability*, Caroline Jarrett and Gerry Gaffney

Chapter 6: Helpful Wayfinding

- *Mental Models*, Indi Young
- Using WAI-ARIA Landmarks, Steve Faulkner: http://rfld.me/19MPhxm

Chapter 7: Clean Presentation

- *Responsive Web Design*, Ethan Marcotte
- Fluid Grid, Ethan Marcotte: http://rfld.me/17sO9RE
- Making Text Legible: Designing for People with Partial Sight, Aries Arditi, Ph.D.: http://rfld.me/19MP9OY
- Dyslexia Style Guide and Typefaces for Dyslexia, British Dyslexia Association: http://rfld.me/1g6LUGB
- Helping Low-vision and Other Users with Web Sites That Meet Their Needs: Is One Site for All Feasible? Mary Theofanos and Janice (Ginny) Redish, in *Technical Communication* 52 (1), 2005
- Tabular Data: Finding the Best Format, Tom Tullis and Stan Fleischman, *Intercom*, June 2004: http://rfld.me/17Ttzod
- Zebra Striping: Does It Really Help? Jessica Enders: http://rfld.me/1eZufgV
- Zebra Striping: More Data for the Case, Jessica Enders: http://rfld.me/1cmwk98
- A Dao of Web Design, John Allsopp: http://rfld.me/1atXO7F

Chapter 8: Plain Language

- *Dynamics in Document Design: Creating Text for Readers*, Karen Schriver
- *Letting Go of the Words: Writing Web Content that Works*, Ginny Redish
- Writing for the Web Versus Writing for Print: Are They Really So Different? Judy Gregory: http://rfld.me/17s1gko
- The Bite, the Snack, and the Meal: How to Feed Content-Hungry Site Visitors, eWrite: http://rfld.me/1cmxxgP

Plain Language Guidelines

- Web Writing Tips, Dey Alexander: http://rfld.me/1dDF5LI
- U.S. Federal Plain Language Guidelines: http://rfld.me/1hmRhRc
- Easy to Read on the Web, Web Accessibility Initiative: www.w3.org/WAI/RD/2012/easy-to-read/Overview.html
- Text Customization for Readability, Web Accessibility Initiative: http://rfld.me/1dhHPvO

Writing for Different Audiences

- More Alike Than You Think, Whitney Quesenbery: http://rfld.me/1cmxlJ0
- Teenagers on the Web, Nielsen Norman Group: http://rfld.me/1aOLy0a
- Designing Web Sites for Older Adults, Ginny Redish and Dana Chisnell: http://rfld.me/1ioMOq3
- Design to Read Guidelines for People Who Do Not Read Easily, Caroline Jarrett, Janice (Ginny) Redish, Kathryn Summers, Kath Straub: www.usabilityprofessionals.org/uxmagazine/people_who_do_not_read_easily/

Chapter 9: Accessible Media

Writing Alternative Text

- Text alternatives for images, 4 Syllables: http://rfld.me/1gVaT0R
- Creating Accessible Images, WebAIM: http://rfld.me/17nAgF1
- HTML5: Techniques for providing useful text alternatives: http://rfld.me/16GfBWL
- Text alternatives for images, Jim Thatcher: http://rfld.me/HoEpMX

Captions and Multimedia Accessibility

- Audio Accessibility: http://rfld.me/1dDzPla
- Accessible Rhetoric: http://rfld.me/1eZsYqa
- Accessible Media Guidelines, National Center for Accessible Media (NCAM): http://rfld.me/1gVaA6o
- Suggested Styles and Conventions for Closed Captioning, WGBH Media Access Group: http://rfld.me/1923hDY

Chapter 10: Universal Usability

- *Flow: The Psychology of Optimal Experience*, Mihaly Csikszentmihalyi
- *Leonardo's Laptop: Human Needs and the New Computing Technologies*, Ben Shneiderman
- *Persuasive Technology: Using Computers to Change What We Think and Do,* B.J. Fogg
- *Seductive Interaction Design: Creating Playful, Fun, and Effective User Experiences*, Stephen P. Anderson
- *Designing the User Interface: Strategies for Effective Human-Computer Interaction*, Ben Shneiderman with Catherine Plaisant, Maxine Cohen, and Steven Jacobs
- Promoting universal usability with multi-layer interface design, Ben Shneiderman: http://rfld.me/1dhCepk
- A Blind User's Profound Review of the iPhone, Austin Seraphin: http://rfld.me/1aALMLJ
- STC Conference Accessibility Guides: How (and Why) They Were Created, Karen Mardahl: http://rfld.me/1dDze9d
- Usable Accessibility: Making Web Sites Work Well for People with Disabilities, Whitney Quesenbery: http://rfld.me/1gVaiMG

Usability Testing

- *Rocket Surgery Made Easy,* Steve Krug
- *The Handbook of Usability Testing,* Dana Chisnell and Jeff Rubin
- *Ready, Set, Test,* Carol Barnum
- Usability Testing Portal, Loop 11/Access Works: www.knowbility. org/v/service-detail/AccessWorks-Usability-Accessibility-Testing-Portal/3k—http://rfld.me/17rXGH8

Chapter 11: Integrated Process

Planning and Project Management

- Accessibility for Project Managers, Henny Swan: www.spotlessinteractive.com/articles/accessibility/accessibility-for-project-managers.php—http://rfld.me/18utJSo

- Accessibility Responsibility Breakdown: www.w3.org/community/wai-engage/wiki/Accessibility_Responsibility_Breakdown—http://rfld.me/1atTp4F

- Canadian Web Accessibility Toolkit: wet-boew.github.com/wet-boew—http://rfld.me/16E4LFL

- WAI Resources on Planning and Implementing Web Accessibility: www.w3.org/WAI/managing.html—http://rfld.me/16Gf2MA

Accessibility Evaluation

- Accessibility evaluation tools, WebAIM: webaim.org/articles/tools/—http://rfld.me/1aAL6FY

- Easy Checks—A First Review of Web Accessibility, Web Accessibility Initiative: www.w3.org/WAI/EO/Drafts/eval/checks—http://rfld.me/18utmaz

- Website Accessibility Conformance Evaluation Methodology (WCAG-EM): www.w3.org/TR/WCAG-EM—http://rfld.me/1g6JTKy

- How to Structure an Accessibility Review, Joe Dolson: www.joedolson.com/articles/2012/01/how-to-structure-an-accessibility-review—http://rfld.me/1aAKLD6

Toolbars to Check Accessibility

- Accessibility Inspector for Firebug: code.google.com/p/ainspector—http://rfld.me/HbS9tL

- WAVE (Firefox): wave.webaim.org/toolbar—http://rfld.me/18usZN5

- Web Accessibility Toolbar (WAT): http://www.paciellogroup.com/resources/wat—http://rfld.me/18usWkq

- Accessibility Evaluation Toolbar (Mozilla): addons.mozilla.org/en-us/firefox/addon/accessibility-evaluation-toolb—http://rfld.me/1eZs5hu

- FireEyes (Deque): www.deque.com/deque-fireeyes—http://rfld.me/17rWMdv

Screen Readers and Screen Magnifiers for Windows

- NonVisual Desktop Access (NVDA): http://rfld.me/1921mPW

- JAWS: http://rfld.me/16gzGWo

- Window-Eyes: http://rfld.me/16gzFIc

- ZoomText Magnifier: http://rfld.me/17rWkvS

- MAGic Screen Magnification: http://rfld.me/1ioGF1Q

Tools to Evaluate Flash and Other Rich Internet Applications

- Microsoft Inspect Objects: http://rfld.me/1ioGq6Z

- aDesigner desktop accessibility tool: http://rfld.me/1cmtpxr

Chapter 12: The Future

- *Design Meets Disability*, Graham Pullin

- *Digital Outcasts: Moving Technology Forward Without Leaving People Behind*, Kel Smith

Index

A

assistive technology
  and need for solid structure, 52
  resources, 247
  universal usability, 203-204
ATAG, 6
attention deficit disorder, 37
attitude (Redish and Chisnell persona
    attributes), 15
audience
  knowing your, 12-13
  plain language, 129
  writing for, 130
audio description, 159-160
autism
  need for helpful wayfinding, 90
  need for plain language, 138
  persona description, 16, 18-19
Autism & Developmental Disability
    Monitoring Network/CDC, 19
automatic speech recognition (ASR), 161
autoplay, 80

B

background
  color contrast to separate foreground
      from, 115-117
  pastel, 116
bar codes, 215
basic literacy level, 131
BBC site, 112
below basic literacy level, 131
Bergel, Marguerite, 72
Berners-Lee, Tim, 64
  machine-readable data, 51
  Worldwide Web Consortium, 6
Biddle, Toby, 194
biodiversity, 2
bites (headline with message), 181
black-and-white control contrast, 115
blindness. *See also* vision disability
  Explore-by-Touch capability, 76
  Google Maps accessibility, 97
  keyboard interaction, 75-78
  need for solid structure, 52

  need for universal usability, 176
  persona description, 16, 22-23
  scanning with ears, 139
  Talking Dialer feature, 78
  video description, 159
  VoiceOver capability, 76
blinking/flashing elements, 164
Boston Globe site, 124
British Standards Institute, 199
Brown, Tim, 8
BrowseAloud technology, 204
Brunelleschi's Dome (King), 43
BS 8878 code of practice, 199
bulleted lists, 133
bullets and tables, 114
buttons, for easy interaction, 69

C

CAPTCHAs, 68
captions, 157, 159
  formatting, 161-162
  style conventions, 162
Career One Stop site, 135
Center for Plain Language, 115, 127
cerebral palsy
  Frankenkindle for people with, 79
  need for simple screen, 40
  need for universal usability, 184
  persona description, 16, 20-21
Chadwick-Dias, Ann, 72
Chisnell, Dana, 15
clean presentation
  for accessibility, 105-106
  ClearRX medication labeling system
      example, 104
  clutter, minimizing, 107-108
  color contrast to separate foreground
      from background, 115-117
  comprehension, design content
      for, 114-115
  customizable design, 108, 112-113
  designing for, 106-119
  first impressions, 108
  flexible grids, 110-111

E

Easy Chirp, 44–45
easy interaction
  for accessibility, 67–69
  accessible instructions and feedback, 72–74
  accordion widget, 70–71
  barriers, 68
  CAPTCHAs, 68
  contingencies, designing for, 80–82
  designing for, 69–82
  error messages, 71
  EZ Access on Amtrak ticket machine example, 66
  failures, 67
  financial service interaction, 72
  guidelines, 220
  HTML code use, 69–70
  importance of, 210
  interface operations, letting users control, 80
  keyboard interaction, 75–78
  large on-screen controls, 78–79
  links and buttons for, 69
  resources, 248
  technology platform features, 71–72
  time-out features, 82
  WAI-ARIA use, 70–71
  WCAG 2.0 and, 83
  WCAG 2.0 resources, 229–232
  who's responsible for, 83
Easy Read, 142
Egger, Sylvia, 42
emphasis tag, 60
Enders, Jessica, 117
equitable use, 7
equivalent use, 43
error messages, 71
  designing for contingencies, 80–82
  providing feedback in response to, 82
Evaluation Methodology Task Force (Eval TF), 203
E-Write, 181
Explore-by-Touch, 76

eye-tracking heatmaps, 137
eye-tracking studies, 108
EZ Access, 66

F

Faulkner, Steve
  wayfinding accessibility, 100–101
Featherstone, Derek
  easy interaction, 85–86
feedback, 72–74
fibromyalgia
  need for easy interaction, 67
  need for helpful wayfinding, 95
  persona description, 16, 24–25
field studies, 185
financial service interaction, 72
finding the way. *See* wayfinding
first impressions, 108
Fisher-Martins, Sandra
  The Right to Understand, 143
Flash
  rich Internet application guidelines, 72
  tab order, 75
flashing/blinking elements, 164
Fleischman, Stan, 117
Fletcher, Valerie, 206–207
Flex, 72
flexibility in use, 7
flexible grids, 110–111
flow, 175
Flow: The Psychology of Optimal Experience (Csikszentmihalyi), 175
fluid grid example page (Marcotte), 111
focus indicator, keyboard interaction, 77
Fogg, B.J., 177
fonts
  color, 116
  customizable design, 112
  easy-to-read, 119
  for people with dyslexia, 121
  Read Regular, 121
  typeface, 119
foreground, color contrast to separate from background, 115–117

forms
    clear purpose support, 37
    interactive feedback, 74
Frankenkindle, 79
future
    accessibility, as part of how we think,
        215–216
    awareness and understanding of
        diverse people, 213–214
    mainstream accessibility, 214–215
    technology innovation, 212–213

G

Gallaudet University/U.S. Census, 27
games, 179–180
Gibson, William, 212
Global Public Inclusive
    Infrastructure, 186
glossaries, 140
Goldberg, Larry
    accessible media, 170–172
Google Maps, 97
graphs, 136
Green, Steve, 213
grids, 110
*A Guide to Good Practice in Commission-
    ing Accessible Websites,* 199

H

hacks, 53
Harris/Interactive/National Association
    on Disability, 21
heading tags
    for easy comprehension, 114
    structural integrity, 53
headings
    lots of (useful), 132
    orientation cues, 93
    structural integrity, 60
helpful wayfinding. *See* wayfinding
Henry, Shawn
    *Just Ask: Integrating Accessibility
        Throughout Design,* 13

Hess, Whitney
    Pleasure and Pain blog, 12
hover actions, keyboard interaction,
    75, 77
HTML (Hypertext Markup Language)
    coding standards and guidelines, 54
    for easy interaction, 69–70
    sectioning markup, 57
HTML5 and ARIA navigation, 95–96
human centered aspect of design
    thinking, 9

I

ICADD (International Committee for
    Accessible Document Design), 63
images, combining links and, 138
inclusive design
    accessibility equation, 4
    clear purpose, 43
information structure, clean
    presentation, 105–106
insight, as design thinking aspect, 9
instructions
    interactive elements, 72–74
    universal usability, 183
integrated practice
    accessibility as way of doing
        business, 193
    accessibility, identifying opportunities
        to integrate, 197
    assessing current knowledge and
        readiness, 198
    assessing what's needed for, 195–198
    commitment to accessibility, 194–195
    guidelines, 223
    media library, 201–202
    policies, setting, 199
    procurement, 202
    resource allocation, 197
    resources, 251–252
    site evaluation, 196
    style guides, 201–202
    supporting an, 198–205
    training, 199

integration, as design thinking aspect, 8

interaction. *See* easy interaction

interface operations

　letting users control, 80

　as support to exploration, 90

intermediate literacy level, 131

International Committee for Accessible
　Document Design (ICADD), 63

iPad, 76

iPhone, 76

iteration, as design thinking aspect, 8

J

Jarrett, Caroline, 214

JavaScript, 54

JAWS screen reader, 60, 204

*Just Ask: Integrating Accessibility Through-
　out Design* (Henry), 13

K

keyboard interaction

　drag and drop, 77

　focus indicator, 77

　hover actions, 75, 77

　keyboard trap, 78

　need for easy interaction, 75–76, 78

　point-and-click, 75–77

　select/activate model of interaction, 77

　tab order, 75

Kindles, 79

King, Ross

　Brunelleschi's Dome, 43

Knowbility organization, 194

L

labels, 69–70

landmarks, wayfinding, 94

language based disability

　need for accessible media, 152

　need for clear purpose site, 38

　need for plain language, 129

　persona description, 17, 30–31

language options. *See also* plain language

　for clean presentation, 115

　customizable design, 112

large on-screen controls, 78–79

layering concept, 181–182

layout grids, 110

leading, 118–119

Leonardo's Laptop (Shneiderman), 3

Lewis, Clayton, 192

Lighthouse/WHO, 29

line breaks, 162

line spacing, 118–119

links

　combining images and, 138

　for easy interaction, 69

　plain language, 138–139

　"read more," 138

　skip, 94

　title, 139

A List Apart article (Marcotte), 110

lists

　bulleted, 133

　and table markup, 114

literacy. *See also* plain language

　levels, 131

　statistics, 131

　types, 132

longdesc attribute, 158

Loop 11 service, 194

low physical effort (Principles of
　Universal Design), 7

lowercase/uppercase text, 119

M

Mace, Ron

　universal design, 7

macular degeneration. *See also* aging
　adults

　need for clean presentation, 106

　need for easy interaction, 74

　persona description, 17, 32–33

Magpie captions editor, 161

mainstream accessibility, 214–215

maintenance, site, 205

usability testing
  moderated sessions, 185
  for plain language, 144
  resources, 250
  for universal usability, 185
user needs, and need for solid
    structure, 52
user research resources, 246

V

Vanderheiden, Gregg, 186
verb use, 133
video description, 159–160
vision disability. *See also* blindness
  customizable design for, 113
  macular degeneration, 32–33,
    74, 106
  need for clean presentation, 114
  persona description, 17, 28–29
visual and semantic space, 117–118
Voice Input, 212
voice recognition, 212
VoiceOver, 76, 178, 204, 212

W

W3C (Worldwide Web Consortium), 6
WAI (W3C Web Accessibility Initia-
    tive), 6, 55
WAI-ARIA
  coding standards and guidelines, 54
  for complex elements, 70–71
  for easy interaction, 70–71
  sectioning markup, 57
WaSP (Web Standards Project), 55
wayfinding
  for accessibility, 90–91
  and aging adults, 92
  airport example, 88
  alternative methods of
    navigation, 96–97
  cues, consistent, 91
  designing for, 91–97
  differentiating things that are
    different, 92–93
  guidelines, 221

importance of, 210
landmarks, 94
orientation cues, 93–94
in real world and online, 89
resources, 248
through consistent elements, 91–92
WCAG 2.0 and, 98–99
WCAG 2.0 resources, 232–233
who's responsible for, 98
WCAG 2.0 (Web Content Accessibility
    Guidelines)
  and accessible media, 167–169
  and clean presentation, 120–122
  coding standards and guidelines, 54
  and easy interaction, 83
  Evaluation Methodology Task Force
    (Eval TF), 203
  and plain language, 145
  POUR principles, 6–7
  requirements in order, 242–243
  and solid structure, 61–62
  and wayfinding, 98–99
Web Accessibility Project, 64
Web Content Accessibility Guidelines.
    See WCAG 2.0
Web Standards Project (WaSP), 55
WebABLE website, 64
wheelchair ramp, 50
white space, 118
Wikipedia, 57
WordPress
  templates, 41–42
  Twenty Ten theme, 41–42
World Health Organization, Census, 23
Worldwide Web Consortium (W3C), 6
Wroblewski, Luke
  Mobile First, 40

Y

"You Are Here" orientation cues, 93
YouTube, 213

Z

Zdenek, Sean, 163
zebra striping, 117

ACKNOWLEDGMENTS

It takes a village to build an accessible website, and just as large and varied a group of people to help us write this book.

The people we profile in the book were generous with their time, often talking to us for several hours, and then later reviewing the book. Thanks to Giles Colborne, Ethan Marcotte, Derek Featherstone, Valerie Fletcher, Steve Faulkner, Larry Goldberg, Mike Paciello, Ginny Redish, and Ben Shneiderman.

We are grateful to Aaron Gustafson for his beautiful foreword, reminding us that for all our technological advances, it all comes down to recognizing everyone's humanity.

Still more people provided valuable feedback, ideas, and assistance in working through the ideas in this book. Thanks to Jimmy Chandler, Dana Chisnell, Gerry Gaffney, Caroline Jarrett, Steve Krug, Jonathan Lazar, Karen Mardahl, Amanda Nance, Daivee Patel, Sharron Rush, Glenda Sims, Julie Strothman, and Jennifer Sutton. Hallway conversations and social media exchanges with too many people to count, let alone mention, helped shape our thoughts over the years. Calls for help to #accessibility on Twitter and the WebAIM discussion group provided fact checks and more ideas.

Thank you, Marta Justak, Lou Rosenfeld, Karen Corbett, Danielle Foster, and everyone at Rosenfeld Media.

The personas were brought to life by Tom Biby, who worked with us to pack a lot of information into a set of small images. Drew Davies also assisted with diagrams and illustrations, making clear concepts out of our scribbles.

Even more people gave us permission to use part of their work in ours, for which we are enormously grateful. They include Deborah Adler, Naomi Alderman, David Andrews, Boér Attila (calcium.ro), Tom Biddle, Ann Chadwick-Dias and Marguerite Bergel, Giles Colborne, Alan Dalton, Drew Davies, Jessica Enders, Lainey Feingold, Sandra Fisher-Martins, B.J. Fogg, Tema Frank, Natascha Frensch, Steve Green, Shawn Lawton Henry, Glenn Johnson, Gunta Klavina, Dennis Lembree, Ethan Marcotte, Michael McAghon, Miguel Neiva, Christopher Phillips, Scotty Reifsnyder,

Cliff Tyllick, Gregg Vanderheiden, Luke Wroblewski, Sean Zdenek.
Organizations also allowed us to use images from their products: A List
Apart, Amara, Apple, Career One Stop, Centers for Medicare & Medicaid
Services, ColorAdd, Commission on a Bill of Rights (UK), CSS Zen
Garden, EasyChirp, Google, IDEO, Microsoft Corporation, Mijkensaar,
Morgan's Wonderland, National Cancer Institute (NCI), National Center
for Accessible Media (NCAM)/WGBH, National Park Services (NPS),
Nomensa, OpenAjax Alliance, OXO, Readability, Simple, Six to Start
and Naomi Alderman, Target, Trace R&D Center, Twitter, University
of Wisconsin-Madison, U.S. Forestry and Wildlife Services, Wikipedia,
WordPress, Zombies, Run!

Sarah Horton

Sarah has spent most of her career working in technology in higher education. She started her career in interaction design in 1991 at the Yale Center for Advanced Instructional Media, creating award-winning interactive instructional software. She was an instructional technologist at Dartmouth College for 11 years before becoming Dartmouth's Director of Web Strategy and Design, leading a team of user-experience professionals responsible for web and media design, development, and production. Most recently Sarah was Web Strategy Project Lead at Harvard University, responsible for strategy and user experience design for the Harvard Web Publishing Initiative.

In the late 1990s, early 2000s, accessibility became part of the discourse when considering strategies for using technology to support teaching and learning. The use of technology is both an opportunity and a potential barrier for students with disabilities. For Sarah, bringing accessibility to the discussion and making design decisions that would improve accessibility gave design and the design process a clear purpose and meaning. She got on board with accessibility and hasn't looked back since.

In 2013 Sarah left higher education to work full-time in accessibility. She joined The Paciello Group, a.k.a. TPG, as Director of Accessible User Experience and Design. In this role she helps leading companies and organizations identify barriers that may keep people with disabilities from getting information, making connections, doing stuff, and learning new things. She helps devise solutions to provide an equitable user experience. She also helps integrate accessibility into practice, through process reviews, training, and usability testing. It is a great time to be working in accessibility, as many companies and organizations are making a commitment to accessibility as a core value, rather than an afterthought.

Sarah is a prolific writer and presenter. She is co-author with Patrick Lynch of *Web Style Guide,* now in its third edition and translated into eight languages. She also wrote *Web Teaching Guide,* which won the American Association of Publishers award for the Best Book in Computer Science in 2000. Her third book, *Access by Design*, combines the disciplines of universal design, accessibility, and usability into guidelines for designing websites that are universally usable. Her publication and presentation credits also include the *New York Times,* Peachpit, and *Digital Web Magazine,* and the International Cross-Disciplinary Workshop on Web Accessibility (W4A), WebVisions, World Usability Day, and the Human-Computer Interaction Laboratory Annual Symposium.

You can find her online at **sarahhortondesign.com** and **@gradualclearing.**

Whitney Quesenbery

Whitney combines a fascination with people and an obsession to communicate clearly with her goal of bringing user research insights to designing products where people matter. She has worked with organizations such as The Open University, National Cancer Institute, Pearson, Sage, Neat, Amtrak, HHS, Apogee, and IEEE.

Her first two books—*Storytelling for User Experience: Crafting Stories for Better Design* (with Kevin Brooks for Rosenfeld Media) and *Global UX: Design and Research in a Connected World* (with Daniel Szuc)—help practitioners keep users in mind throughout the creative process.

She's also passionate about civic design. As co-director of the non-profit Center for Civic Design with Dana Chisnell, she works with election officials on usability and design of ballots and other election materials. They publish the popular *Field Guides to Ensuring Voter Intent,* which provide researched guidelines in a handy pocket format. Their work is funded by the MacArthur Foundation, the James Irvine Foundation, and the National Science Foundation.

Whitney is a co-author of two influential Brennan Center reports that show just how much design matters in elections. From 2004 to 2009, she was chair for Human Factors and Privacy for the Elections Assistance Commission's committee developing voting system guidelines.

Her interest in accessibility and civic design came together when she served as UPA's representative on the Access Board's advisory committee, drafting updates for the U.S. "Section 508" accessibility regulations. She managed an EAC grant for accessible voting technology that brought together researchers and election officials in a dozen projects, including the influential *Anywhere Ballot* and an OpenIDEO design challenge.

Whitney has been part of events and publications around the world, including World Usability Day, User Friendly, Fluxible, Agile, UXPA, STC, SIG-CHI, CSUN, AccessU, Web Accessibility Initiative research symposia, PlainTalk, UX Australia, the Accessibility Summit, and has given testimony for the Presidential Commission on Election Administration.

Before she was seduced by a little, beige computer into software, usability, and interface design, Whitney was a theatrical lighting designer on and off Broadway, learning about storytelling from some of the masters.

Follow Whitney's practical UX advice anytime on Twitter @whitneyq.